THE BOOK OF BOSTON

Old State House, showing the balcony from which the Declaration of Independence was first read in Boston

The Book of
BOSTON

THE COLONIAL PERIOD
1630 to 1775

By MARJORIE DRAKE ROSS

With photographs by Samuel Chamberlain

HASTINGS HOUSE PUBLISHERS

New York

To

MY HUSBAND

John Clifford Ross

AND MY SON

John Drake Ross

This Book is
Affectionately Inscribed

Published simultaneously in Canada
by S. J. Reginald Saunders, Publishers, Toronto 2B.

Library of Congress Catalog Card Number: 60-9122

Printed in the United States of America

CONTENTS

List of Illustrations 9
Preface 15
Acknowledgments 17
The Book of Boston 19
    Explorers 26
    Colonies 26
    Early Wooden Houses 28
    The Colonial South End 31
    Old Boston 32
    The North End 40
    Old Boston Streets 47
    The Great Fires 49
    The Paul Revere House 51
    Other Famous Early American Buildings 55
    The Beacon 56
    Provincial Boston 56
    Other Brick Houses 61
    Taverns 71
    Other Colonial Brick Buildings 75
    The Old State House 95
    Independence 98
    King's Chapel 100
    Other Burial Grounds 105
    Colonial Houses on Beacon Street 108
A suggested tour of Colonial Boston for the hurried, intelligent traveler 121
Map of Colonial Boston with historic sites 122
Some historic sites near Boston 123
Index 125

The TOWN of BOSTON

IN

New England

by

Capt John Bonner

1722

Ætatis Suæ 60.

Engraved from a copy in the possession of Wm Taylor Esq.
and published by
GEORGE G. SMITH & VGRAITH
1867 No 91 Washington opposite State Street Boston.
1835.

I have examined this plan and f
copy of the original
Boston July 2 1835 —

Roxbury Flatts

West Hill

Fox Hill

Beacon H

PowderHouse

Watch House

COMMON

Garden

School St

Newbury

Orange Str

From Town H.
One Mile

Orange Str

Pond

Goals
Garden

Rainford L

Pond Str

Fortification

Wind Mill Point

Hills Wharfe

Derby W

Batte W

Scale of ¼ a Mile.

BOSTON : N.E.

Planted An. Dom 1630

A. The Old Church	1630
B. Old North	1650
C. Old South	1660
D. Annabaptist	1680
E. Chh of England	1688
F. Brattle St Church	1699
G. Quakers	1710
H. New North	1714
I. New South	1716
K. French	1716
L. New Wm Brick	1721

EXPLANATION.

a. Town House.	
b. Governours House.	
c. South Gramar School.	
d. North Gramar School.	
e. Writing School.	
f. Writing School.	
g. Alms House.	
h. Bridewell.	
Streets 42 Lanes 36 Alleys 22	
Houses near 3000.	
1000 Brick rest Timber.	
Near 12000 People.	

Great Fires.

First	1653
Second	1676
Third	1679
Fourth	1683
Fifth	1690
Sixth	1691
Seventh	1702
Eigth	1711

Gen¹
Small Pox.

First	1640
Second	1660
Third	1677 1678
Fourth	1689 1690
Fifth	1702
Sixth	1721

Engraven and P

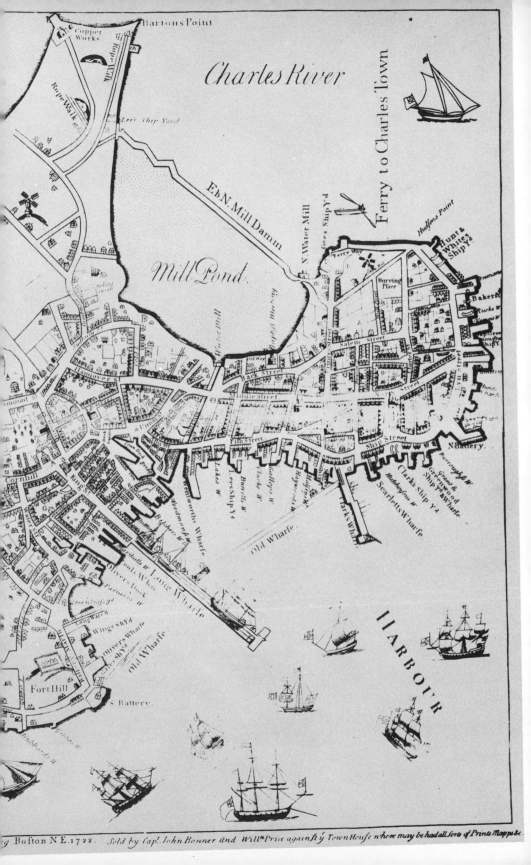

Barton's Point

Charles River

Copper Works

RopeWalk

Ler's Ship Yard

Eb N. Mill Damm

N Water Mill

Gees Ship Yd

Ferry Way

Hudsons Point

Hunt & Whites Ship Yd

Mill Pond.

Watermill

Burying Place

Baker

Rucks W

Ship

Salem Street

Old Way

Hanover

Black Street

Middle Street

Ship Street

N Battery

Cornhill

King

Fleet Street

Union

Burroughs W
Greenwood
Clarks Ship Prt & Wharfe
Hutchinsons W
Scarletts Wharfe

Wentworths Wharfe

Lakes W
Clerks W
Bussells W
Hallyes W
Haywards W

Clarks Wharf

Butchers Wd

Old Wharfe

Oliver's Whar

Long Wharfe

Greenleaf Yd
Long Wharf
Wings shYd
Olivers Wharfe
old Wharfe

Fort Hill

S. Battery

HARBOUR

LIST OF ILLUSTRATIONS

Old State House, showing the balcony from which the
Declaration of Independence was first read in Boston   Frontis

Bonner's Map of Boston 1722   6, 7

Exterior of the 17th century Saugus Ironworks house   20

Interior showing the fireplace   21

Captain John Smith's Map of New England 1614
    Courtesy, New York City Public Library, New York   22

Portrait of John Winthrop, first governor of the Massachusetts
Bay Colony (1588-1649) — Artist Unknown
    *Courtesy, Art Commission of the Commonwealth of
    Massachusetts*   24

The Mayflower II   27

Exterior of a typical 17th century thatched dwelling-house
A reproduction in the Pioneers' Village, Salem   29

Benjamin Franklin's Birthplace as shown in Caleb Snow's
History of Boston, 1828
    *Courtesy, The Society for the Preservation of New England
    Antiquities*   30

Boston and Castle Island — about 1638 — View from Charlestown
    Courtesy, The Boston Athenaeum   33

The First Graveyard — beside King's Chapel.
Some of the oldest stones   34

The Winthrop Cup. A standing cup marked London 1610
    *Courtesy, The First Church of Boston and the Museum of
    Fine Arts, Boston*   35

Boston Common   36

The First Town House (1657-1711)
Courtesy, The Bostonian Society   37

Map of Boston, showing The Neck and the islands in the harbor
Courtesy, The Bostonian Society   38

The Paul Revere House restored to the 17th century building   41

Copp's Hill Burying Ground. Old heraldic stones
*Courtesy, The Society for the Preservation of New England
Antiquities*   42

Mather Tomb
Courtesy, Richard Merrill   43

Pine Tree Shilling — Massachusetts. The first coins made in
New England
Courtesy, the Museum of Fine Arts, Boston   44

Old Streets Plan. The largest area in downtown Boston retaining
the 17th century layout of streets, lanes and alleys
Courtesy, Boston National Historic Sites Commission   45

The Boston Stone, marking the center of the town
Courtesy, Richard Merrill   46

The Old North Church in North Square, built 1677
Courtesy, The Boston Athenaeum   48

Portrait of Cotton Mather (1663-1728) by Peter Pelham
Courtesy, The Museum of Fine Arts, Boston   50

Portrait of Judge Samuel Sewall (1688-1751) by John Smibert
Courtesy, The Museum of Fine Arts, Boston   51

List of Illustrations

The Paul Revere House, end view, restored to the 17th
century style
Courtesy, Richard Merrill   52

The Paul Revere House — of three stories, as it was when he
lived in it in the 18th century. Photograph by W. A. French
about 1880 before the restoration
*Courtesy, The Society for the Preservation of New England
Antiquities*   53

The Old Feather Store, Dock Square, from a stereograph of 1860
*Courtesy, The Society for the Preservation of New England
Antiquities*   54

The First King's Chapel, built 1689, enlarged 1710, showing the
wooden building and the beacon pole on Beacon Hill
Courtesy, The Bostonian Society   55

The Old Province House, from a drawing originally owned
by F. H. Manning
Courtesy, The Bostonian Society   57

The Indian Archer Weathervane from the Old Province House
by Shem Drowne
Courtesy, The Massachusetts Historical Society   59

The Moses Pierce-Hichborn House, 1711, North Square
Courtesy, Richard Merrill   62

An interior view of the Hichborn House showing the staircase
Courtesy, Richard Merrill   63

The Capen House, built about 1714   65

Birthplace of Count Rumford, Woburn — 1714   66

The oldest shoe store in Boston   68

The Ebenezer Hancock House
Courtesy, Richard Merrill   69

The Blue Ball
Shop sign of Benjamin Franklin's father   70

The Green Dragon Tavern, Union Street, where the Boston
Tea Party was planned
   Courtesy, The Boston Athenaeum   71

Early Newspaper, *The New England Courant*, published
in Boston
   Courtesy, The Bostonian Society   73

The Old Corner Bookstore, built about 1712
   Courtesy, The Boston Athenaeum   74

Southeast view of Boston by William Price, 1743, showing the
ships and church steeples   76, 77

Exterior of Christ Church, Salem Street. Old photograph
taken from Hull Street   79

Interior of Christ Church, now called the "Old North Church,"
showing the box pews and the chandeliers   80

Interior of Christ Church showing the organ loft   81

Exterior of the Old South Meeting house, built 1729, replacing
an earlier wooden meeting house   83

The Harris Pitcher by Ebenezer Moulton, 1810, showing
the Old South Meeting house on fire.
   Courtesy, The Museum of Fine Arts, Boston   84

The original Faneuil Hall, 1742
   *Courtesy, The Society for the Preservation of New England
Antiquities*   87

The Grasshopper Weathervane on Faneuil Hall by Shem Drowne
   Courtesy, The Bostonian Society   88

List of Illustrations

Portrait of Peter Faneuil by John Smibert
Courtesy, The Massachusetts Historical Society   91

First page of Peter Faneuil's Household Inventory, 1743
Courtesy, Suffolk County Probate Records, Boston   93

Detail of the Old State House, the English Lion and the Unicorn   95

Exterior of the Old State House   97

Exterior of King's Chapel, the stone building erected in 1749   99

Interior of King's Chapel, the organ loft   101

Interior of King's Chapel, the box pews, columns and pulpit   102

Interior of King's Chapel, the colonial governor's pew restored   103

The Old Granary Burying Ground, the oldest stones and tombs   106

The Central Burying Ground—on the Common, old stones
and wall tombs.
Courtesy, Richard Merrill   106

Gilbert Stuart plaque
*Courtesy, The Society for the Preservation of New England
Antiquities*   107

Portrait of John Hancock (1737-1815) by John Singleton Copley
Courtesy, The Museum of Fine Arts, Boston   108

Portrait of Mercy Otis Warren (1728-1814) by
John Singleton Copley
Courtesy, The Museum of Fine Arts, Boston   109

View of the Common, 1708, after a water color by Christian
Remick engraved by Sidney Smith, 1904, showing the Hancock
House and the beacon on Beacon Hill
　　Courtesy, The Bostonian Society. The original is owned by
　　the Concord Antiquarian Society　　　　　　　　　　　111

18th century Colonial interior of *Mount Pleasant*, Philadelphia,
of the type also found in Boston at this time
　　Courtesy, Pennsylvania Museum of Art, Philadelphia　　112

18th century Colonial Staircase in the Derby House, Salem, of the
type also used in Boston at this time
　　Courtesy, The Derby House, Salem　　　　　　　　　113

Shirley Place, a Colonial Governor's Mansion, built 1748 by
Governor William Shirley on Roxbury Hill
　　Courtesy, Boston National Historic Sites Commission
　　This perspective for restoration drawn by Edgar J. P. Walker　114

Entrance door at *Shirley Place*　　　　　　　　　　　　115

Window seat at *Shirley Place*　　　　　　　　　　　　116

Liberty Tree, 1774, from an old print.
　　*Courtesy, The Society for the Preservation of New England
　　Antiquities*　　　　　　　　　　　　　　　　　　117

Portrait of Paul Revere (1734-1818) by John Singleton Copley
　　Courtesy, The Museum of Fine Arts, Boston　　　　　118

The Liberty Bowl by Paul Revere
　　Courtesy, The Museum of Fine Arts, Boston　　　　　119

The Liberty Tree plaque, site of the Liberty Tree, on a building
at the end of Boylston Street on Washington Street
　　Courtesy, Richard Merrill　　　　　　　　　　　　120

MAP of colonial Boston, with historic sites indicated　　　122

PREFACE

MORE THAN one hundred years ago, in midwinter of 1842, Boston received a visit from a celebrated English tourist, the novelist Charles Dickens. He wrote later in his *American Notes* that having arrived late Saturday night he could not see the town, but was out early the next morning eager for first impressions. "When I got into the streets upon this Sunday morning," he wrote, "the air was so clear, the houses were so bright and gay, the sign-boards were painted in such gaudy colors, the gilded letters were so very golden, the bricks were so very red, the stone was so very white, the blinds and area railings were so very green, the knobs and plates upon the street-doors so marvellously bright and twinkling . . . that every thoroughfare in the city looked exactly like a scene in a pantomime." "The city is a beautiful one," he continued, "and cannot fail, I should imagine, to impress all strangers very favorably." And so it has down through the years.

As late as 1842 there was much of seventeenth- and eighteenth-century Boston left for Mr. Dickens to see. The Province and Hancock houses and the Old Feather Store, to mention but three famous landmarks, were still very much a part of the picture. During the past century, however, there have been many changes with more promised for the future, and it is important to know what remains. For the modern visitor who, like Charles Dickens, sets out to gather his own impressions, and for the "armchair tourist," this book on Boston's many landmarks, past and present, will make a more meaningful sojourn. Most important of all, the book shows how the seemingly isolated landmarks and the museum exhibitions of today fit together to make for us a very real "pantomime" of Boston's past.

Abbott Lowell Cummings

Assistant director of the Society for the Preservation of New England Antiques. Formerly assistant curator of the American Wing, the Metropolitan Museum, New York.

ACKNOWLEDGMENTS

THE FOLLOWING sources have been drawn upon in the compiling of this book. The author is very grateful and indebted to them.

Comer, William R., *Landmarks in the Old Bay State*. Norwood: Norwood Press, 1911.

Crawford, Mary Caroline, *Little Pilgrimages Among Old New England Inns*. Boston: L. C. Page Company, 1907.

Crawford, Mary Caroline, *Old Boston in Colonial Days or St. Botolph's Town*. Boston: L. C. Page Company, 1908.

Drake, Samuel Adams, *Old Landmarks and Historic Personages of Boston*. Boston: James R. Osgood, 1875.

Duane, C. W., *Christ Church Boston*. William Carrie, 1901.

Foote, Henry W., *Annals of King's Chapel*. Boston: Little, Brown and Company, 1887.

Forbes, Esther, *Paul Revere and the World He Lived In*. Boston: Houghton Mifflin Company, 1942.

Howe, M. A. De Wolfe, *Boston Landmarks*. New York: Hastings House, 1947.

Mann, Albert W., *Walks and Talks about Historic Boston*. Boston: Mann Publishing Company, 1917.

Shackleton, Robert, *The Book of Boston*. Philadelphia: Penn Publishing Company, 1916.

Stark, James H., *Stark's Antique Views of ye Towne of Boston*. James H. Stark, 1901.

Tercentenary Exercises, *The General Court of Massachusetts 1630-1930*. Boston: Wright and Potter Legislative Printers, 1930.

Thwing, Annie Haven, *The Crooked and Narrow Streets of Boston*. Boston: Marshall Jones Company, 1920.

Whitehill, Walter Muir, *Boston, A Topographical History*. Cambridge: The Belknap Press of Harvard University Press, 1959.

Whitmore, William H., *Old State House Memorial*. City of Boston, 1883.

Winsor, Justin, *The Memorial History of Boston*. Boston: James R. Osgood Company, 1883.

Young, Alexander, *Chronicles of the First Planters of the Colony of Massachusetts Bay*. Boston: Charles Little and James Brown, 1846.

Sincere thanks are due for the valuable assistance of Jean P. Colby, Elizabeth Cash and Abbott Lowell Cummings.

MARJORIE DRAKE ROSS

The Book of
BOSTON

THE COLONIAL PERIOD
1630 to 1775

BOSTON, whichever way you turn, awakens curiosity and interest. This small volume cannot possibly include all of its famous places or cover completely its architecture and history. In it, however, you will visit the most significant of these spots and will see what a great contribution Boston has made to our heritage.

There is no other major city in the country, with the possible exception of Philadelphia, where there are so many important colonial sites and where so many early buildings may be seen still standing in their original settings as in Boston. With many of its narrow crooked streets surviving, the north end of the city is a priceless relic of seventeenth century colonial town planning. The early Bostonians have left their mark on history, too. From this old town came the strong, sincere men who played important

Exterior of the 17th century Saugus Ironworks house

Interior showing the fireplace

parts in the development of our country and established many of the great educational and industrial organizations that form the backbone of our culture. The founding of Harvard College, only six years after the settlement was established, and the building of the blast furnace, forge, and mill at the ** ironworks in Saugus before the middle of the seventeenth century are but two evidences of this.

* Historic site or building now standing.
** Historic site or building open to visitors.

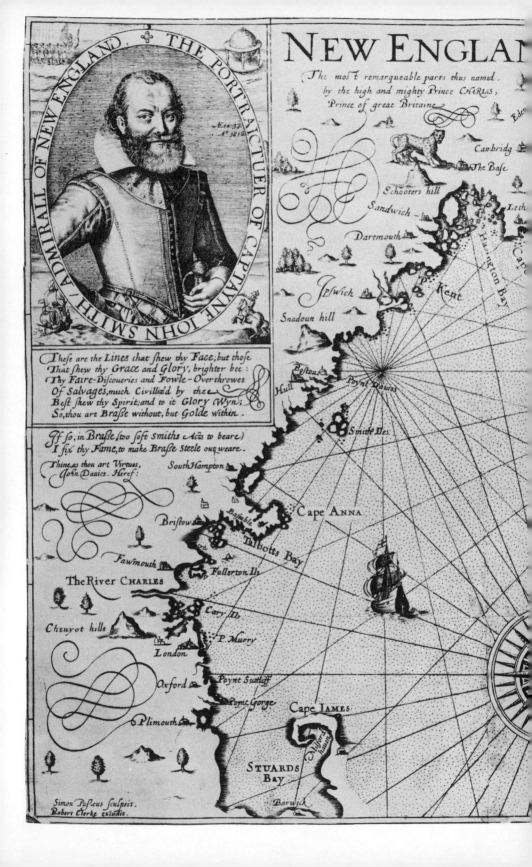

THE PORTRAICTUER OF CAPTAYNE IOHN SMITH ADMIRALL OF NEW ENGLAND.

Æta: 37. Aᵒ 1616.

NEW ENGLAN

The most remarqueable parts thus named.
by the high and mighty Prince CHARLES,
Prince of great Britaine

These are the Lines that shew thy Face; but those
That shew thy Grace and Glory, brighter bee:
Thy Faire-Discoueries and Fowle-Overthrowes
Of Salvages, much Civilliz'd by thee
Best shew thy Spirit; and to it Glory Wyn:
So, thou art Brasse without, but Golde within.

If so; in Brasse (too soft Smiths Acts to beare)
I fix thy Fame, to make Brasse steele out weare.
Thine as thou art Virtues,
John Dauies. Heref:

Edc

Cambridg

The Base

Leth

Schooters hill

Sandwich

Dartmouth

Hamton Bay

Cap

Ipswich

P. Kent

Snadoun hill

Beston

Hull

Poynt Dauies

Smith Iles.

SouthHampton

Bristow

Bassable

Cape ANNA

Fawmouth

Talbotts Bay

The River CHARLES

Fullerton Ils.

Cary Ils.

Cheuyot hills

P. Murry

London

Oxford

Poynt Sutliff

Poynt Gorge

Cape IAMES

Plimouth

Milford haven

STUARDS BAY

Barwick

Simon Passeus sculpsit.
Robert Clerke excudit.

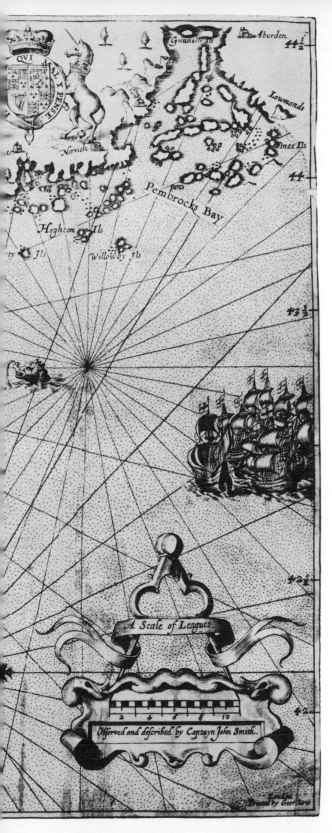

*Captain John Smith's
Map of New England
1614*

23

Portrait of John Winthrop, first governor of the Massachusetts Bay Colony (1588-1649) — Artist Unknown

In 1630 John Winthrop and his little band of Puritans, including Richard Saltonstall and Lady Arbella Johnson, landed in * Salem, about fifteen miles north of Boston. During the long, weary twenty-six-day voyage, attended by all the "perils of the deep," Winthrop wrote in his journal the beginnings of his history of New England, an important account of life in this part of the country.

Soon these early Puritans of the Massachusetts Bay Company moved on and established themselves on a small peninsula in Boston Harbor between the Mystic and the Charles rivers in what is now Charlestown. Here they discovered that there was a lack of good fresh water as Edward Johnson records in his *Wonder Working Providence*: "They could find but one Spring, and that not to be come by but when the tide was down."

The Reverend William Blackstone (or Blaxton) who had come over earlier with Robert Gorges' expedition in 1623 had remained when most of the others in that party had returned to England. In 1625 he became the first white settler of Boston. Here he lived as a hermit in the vicinity of what is now Louisburg (pronounced Looisburg) Square on Beacon Hill. He had title to a large tract of land on which he had his dwelling-hut, a garden, and an excellent spring.

At the invitation of the Reverend Blackstone, Winthrop and his small colony moved from Charlestown and settled along the present Washington Street, between Milk and State streets, where they found a "Sweet spring" in what is today still called Spring Lane. As Alexander Young in his *Chronicles of the First Planters of the Colony of Massachusetts Bay* says: "whither also the frame of the Governor's house was also (to the discontent of some) carried; where people began to build their houses against winter; and this place was called Boston."

Explorers

Boston was founded in 1630 but several explorers had come earlier. Among them were John Cabot and his three sons, who set sail in 1497 in ships outfitted by Henry VII to establish England's right of possession in what is now New England. The next year one of these sons, John Cabot the Younger, returned and skirted the coast line from Newfoundland to Florida.

Captain John Smith in 1614 sailed along the shore of North America and into what was to be Boston Harbor. He named the environs New England and drew a famous map of this area.

Colonies

The Pilgrims landed on these shores in 1620 seeking religious freedom. They established the first permanent settlement in New England at *Plymouth on Massachusetts Bay about forty miles south of the present site of Boston. They had sailed from Plymouth, England, in the one-hundred-and-eighty-ton *Mayflower*. In 1957 the voyage was made again in a replica of this famous little ship. This ** *Mayflower II* is now berthed at Plymouth, Massachusetts, where it is one of the exhibits of the ** Plimoth Plantation. This Plantation is a reproduction of the old Pilgrim village which includes the Fort Meetinghouse and several homes furnished in the seventeenth century manner. All of these are open to visitors.

The Mayflower II

Early Wooden Houses

The first dwellings for the most part were small rectangular frame houses with thatched pitched roofs and an end chimney. In each one there was a batten entrance door and usually two or three small casement windows with diamond-shaped panes.

There was generally one room with an attic above where the children slept. This was reached by a ladder and warmed by the chimney. The room on the ground floor was called the "hall" as it was in England and served as a living-dining room for the family. The great fireplace filled one end of this room and here all the cooking was done in iron utensils, most of which were made at the Saugus ironworks.

There was little furniture in these halls, perhaps one armchair and some joint stools, a table, and a frame bed for the parents, which was folded up against the wall when not in use. There was always the family Bible and a wheel for spinning. These small wooden huts were our first type of colonial house.

Exterior of a typical 17th century thatched dwelling-house
A reproduction in the Pioneers' Village, Salem

Benjamin Franklin's Birthplace as shown in Caleb Snow's
History of Boston, *1828*

The
Colonial South End

Very soon, however, and throughout the seventeenth century, larger houses were built of wooden clapboards with shingled roofs, gables, and overhanging upper stories. One of these was the birthplace of Benjamin Franklin. It was rented by his father in 1685 and destroyed by fire in 1810. A plaque now marks the site on Milk Street.

Many of these early homesteads are mentioned in the *Book of Possessions*, an early town record book of Boston written about 1645 containing the names of some two hundred and forty of the first settlers. Maps of early Boston were drawn from information in this unique volume, which was later copied and published by the city. The original is now in safekeeping in Boston City Hall.

Among these early settlers of the Massachusetts Bay Colony were about one hundred university men from England who settled in, or very close to Boston between 1630 and 1647. Many were ministers but others were professional men. Boston was learned from the beginning.

Old Boston

The old Indian name of pre-colonial Boston was Shawmut, said to mean "Living Waters." The original Shawmut was a small, wide peninsula connected to the mainland by a very narrow neck. There were about seven hundred and eighty-three acres indented deeply by coves and almost surrounded by water. In the center were three hills: Trimountain, Copp's Hill, and Fort Hill. The Trimountain had three peaks known as Pemberton, Beacon, and Mount Vernon.

32

Boston and Castle Island — about 1638
View from Charlestown

On September 17, 1630, at Charlestown, the Court of Assistants with Governor Winthrop presiding voted "That the Trimountaine shall be called Boston." This name, taken from Boston or Saint Botolph's Town in Lincolnshire, England, was dear to their hearts as many had migrated from there.

Colonial Boston grew in the pattern of the old English villages, with a meetinghouse, market square, and dwelling houses. These were connected by narrow lanes, byways, and a few highways as early as 1636. There was also one cemetery. This was the * graveyard now beside

The First Graveyard besides King's Chapel. Some of the oldest stones

King's Chapel. It was located there in 1630 on the lot of Sir Isaac Johnson, who requested that he be buried on his own land. Others were interred near him and this became the oldest and for thirty years the only burying ground in Boston. It was mentioned by Samuel Sewall, the well-known witch-trial judge in his diary. This valuable record of the colonial period from 1673 to 1729 contained many references to important people and events. It may be found among the papers at the Massachusetts Historical Society.

The original meetinghouse, which was the first building used by the First Church of Boston, was built on the main street originally named King's Street but changed to State Street after the Revolutionary War. To this church,

The Winthrop Cup.
A standing cup
marked London 1610

which was then Congregational, now Unitarian, Governor Winthrop presented a handsome silver "standing cup" made in London in 1610 to be used as a communion vessel. ** It is now on loan to the Boston Museum of Fine Arts where it may be seen.

This wooden thatched building served until 1640 when a new wooden church was built nearby on what is now Washington Street at the head of State Street. There the General Court met from 1644 to 1657.

The lot in front of the meetinghouse was set apart for a market place. Here the whipping post, pillory, and stocks were placed. Close by was the town pump where public notices were posted.

In 1634 the early settlers bought forty-five acres of land from William Blackstone, the hermit, paying him thirty pounds. This they set apart for "Common use." It

35

Boston Common

remains so today as * Boston Common, the oldest park in
the country. A law of 1640 states: "There shall be no
land granted either for house plott or garden out of ye
open ground or Common field." Here the militia drilled
and the cattle grazed and drank from the pond known
now as the Frog Pond.

36

In 1657 the first Town House was built at the head of King's Street, now the site of the old State House. A legacy of three hundred pounds from Captain Robert Keayne, a tailor and the first commander of the Ancient and Honorable Artillery, with added subscriptions, provided the necessary funds. Some contributed in "Corne, country pay, in goods, provisions or wheat," and others listed on the town record agreed "to give in hats, or pay in brick lyeme or three dayes worke."

The Town House was another colonial interpretation of the English medieval style of architecture with gables and overhanging upper stories but built of wood instead of half-timber. It was set up on twenty-one pillars, each ten feet high, which supported the overhanging stories.

BOSTON'S FIRST TOWN-HOUSE
1657~1711

The First Town House (1657-1711)

37

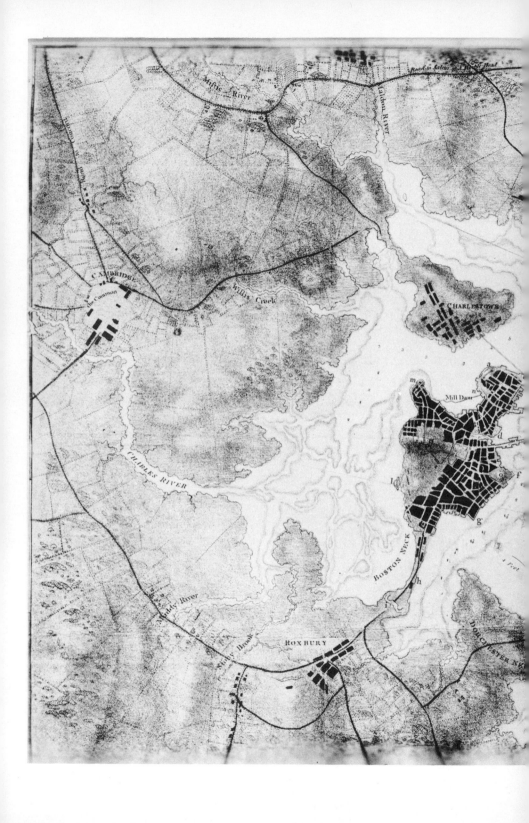

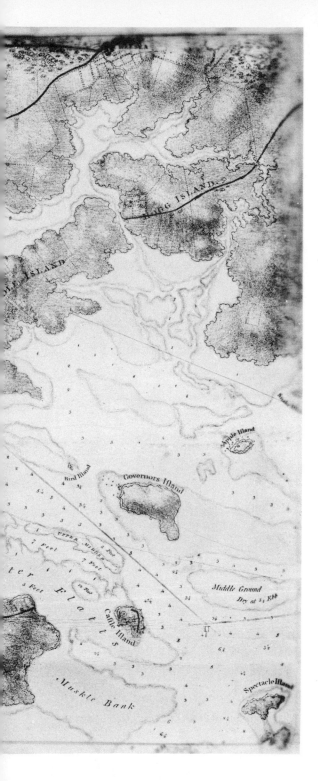

*Map of Boston, showing
The Neck and the islands
in the harbor*

39

There were two towers and a balustraded walk on the roof. The ground floor had open shops for the merchants, and above were the chambers used by the General Court for their monthly meetings. In 1659 the selectmen of Boston voted that "no one should smoke or bring a fire or match, under or about, the Town House," but in spite of these precautions it burned in 1711 in the "great fire." This old wooden building was replaced in 1712 by the present brick colonial one which after the Revolution was known as the old State House.

The earliest center of the settlement was this colonial South End. It stretched along Cornhill Street and King's Street, now Washington and State streets. Beyond was the water front and Fort Hill (now leveled), where the old fort stood looking out over the harbor.

The North End

The North End was the next to develop. This area, also rich in history, proudly displays the only remaining seventeenth-century house in Boston, still standing on its original site. It is known as the ** Paul Revere House because Paul Revere and his family lived there a century later. (See pages 51-54 for further details of this house.)

At this time other colonial homes and wharves fringed the water front and looked out over the green wooded islands in the harbor. Shops were nearby on the wharves or in the ground-floor rooms of the houses.

The Paul Revere House restored to the 17th century building

Swinging from brackets attached to their walls were decorative signs with pictures or symbols of the trade carried on within. *A king's head and looking glass* hung where William Price sold prints and maps. Daniel Parker, a goldsmith, had a *Golden Ball*, a shoemaker a *sign of the Boot*, a hatter a sign with a "Hatt and a Beaver," and a drygoods shop displayed the "Sign of the Stay."

North was Copp's Hill, supposed to have been named for an early settler, William Copp, a cordwainer or shoemaker from Stratford-on-Avon in England, who had his dwelling there. This is mentioned in the *Book Of Possessions* and his will is on file in the Probate Office for the County of Suffolk. Copp's Hill was sometimes called Snow Hill and also Mill Field because of the windmill

Copp's Hill Burying Ground. Old heraldic stones

Mather Tomb

erected on it in 1634. This was the first windmill in Boston
and was used for grinding corn. Brought from Cambridge
where it would not turn for lack of wind, it was set up on
this breezy summit and worked very well. Also, ** the
second burying ground, which was first used in 1661, was
laid out on Copp's Hill. Still to be seen, shaded by great
trees, are many early gravestones with quaint inscriptions.
There are also fine armorial markers set in the west wall.
Among the famous early Bostonians who lie here are the
two ministers Increase and his son Cotton Mather.

    Running beside the cemetery is Hull Street, named
for John Hull, the colonial silversmith, who with Robert
Sanderson made the first silver coins in New England.
These coins, known as the Pine Tree shillings, were pro-

duced in the mint authorized by the General Court in 1652 and established in Hull's house. On one side of these coins was a pine tree and the word "Massachusetts" and on the other the date 1652 and the words "New England." The dies for these were designed by Joseph Jenks of Lynn, our first ironfounder, ** whose works have been mentioned in Saugus. Hannah Hull, wife of Judge Sewall, gave some of her father's land in this neighborhood for ** the way still called by his name.

At the foot of Copp's Hill was the ferry to Charlestown which began carrying the colonists across the Charles River in 1631. Later there were many shipyards along this shore on the Boston side and opposite on the Charlestown water front the Navy Yard was set up in the late eighteenth century. It was also here that Paul Revere rowed across from Boston to Charlestown to begin his famous ride.

The hill was higher than it is now and from the top there was an unbroken view of Charlestown and the harbor. In 1807 much of Copp's Hill was cut down to fill in the Mill Pond, now the North Station area.

The colonial Town Dock stood at the head of Town Cove, now the Quincy Market district. This cove cut in

Pine Tree Shilling — Massachusetts. The first coins made in New England

44

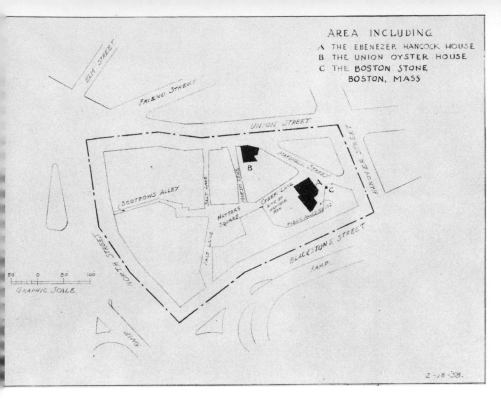

Old Streets Plan. The largest area in downtown Boston retaining the 17th century layout of streets, lanes and alleys

between Fort Hill and Copp's Hill and divided the North and South ends of the town.

The old seventeenth-century narrow streets, alleys, and lanes in this part of Boston, although sometimes inconvenient, form a unique layout and are a priceless heritage which should be preserved. Like so much of the North End, they are picturesque byways with quaint names such as Marsh Lane, Green Lane, and Salt Lane. Most of them received their names before 1708 and retain them today. In 1665 Creek Square was part of the colonial Mill Creek. Marshall Street was laid out by Thomas Marshall in 1667 and led to the colonial Town Dock, which is now Dock Square. Today it is about a half mile inland.

45

The Boston Stone, marking the center of the town.

Here at the corner of Marshall Street and Creek Lane was placed the ** Boston Stone. This was considered the central landmark. No one knows why this stone was used as a marker except that it was available. Brought from England in 1635, this ancient stone was originally a paint millstone. It was used for grinding pigments by rolling the ball-shaped stone back and forth in the trough to which it is now attached. These powdered pigments were mixed with linseed oil to make paint. The date on the stone is thought

46

to have been added by an alehouse owner in the neighbor-hood who wished to imitate the London Stone, an old Roman stone that marks the center of London.

The paint mill, to which this stone belonged, was the property of Thomas Child, an early Boston painter of note, mentioned by Judge Sewall in his diary. Mr. Child bought part of the Marshall estate at the corner of Marshall and Union streets near where the stone now stands. In 1701, he placed over the shop door of this house a coat of arms of the ancient guild of painters and over this a shield with the initials "T.K." for Thomas and Katherine, his wife who worked with him, probably preparing the paints. This ** colonial painter's arms sign may be seen in the collection of the Bostonian Society at the Old State House.

As early as 1706 Thomas Child did fancy house painting and interior work such as graining to imitate cedar wood and marble. He may have painted portraits as well. Among the colors used at that time on colonial woodwork were Dutch pink, Prussian blue, olive green, and Indian red, colors much in favor today.

Old Boston Streets

The old colonial lanes were four feet wide with the exception of the main streets or highways, which were six feet. Few were paved and all were without sidewalks. Some, however, such as the fashionable Clark Square in the North End, were paved with cobblestones brought up

from the beaches. Ann Street was laid out in 1649 and led
to North Square, which was called Clark Square until
1758. This was never a square but was triangular in shape.
It was the center of the second settlement of early Boston.

The Old North Church in North Square, built 1677

The Great Fires

Fire was one of the horrors of these early days and Boston suffered from a series of them. The first was in 1653 and by 1711 there had been eight. Every family had fire buckets of leather hanging in the entry but these were of small size and worth little against the raging flames. Many of the earliest fires started in the chimneys. At first these were built of wood siding or logs and clay. Finally, fieldstone and brick, which were more fireproof, replaced them.

After the great fire of 1676 in the North End, many dwellings and meetinghouses were built there. Later wharves, shops, and taverns sprang up. All were connected by crooked lanes and byways with a few highways leading to the water front. The ways about the new north meetinghouse were laid out and known as Sun Court, Moon Court, and Bell Alley.

The Second Church of Boston was the original old North Church, built in 1650. Rebuilt in 1677 after the fire, it became known as the Mather church as both Increase and his son Cotton Mather served as its ministers. Along with some one hundred other buildings this wooden meetinghouse was torn down by the British soldiers during the Revolutionary War and used for firewood.

In 1799 the members of this church in North Square, being without a meetinghouse, joined the NEW Brick Church also in the North End. This meetinghouse, on

Middle Street, also known as the "Cockerel" Church because of its cock on the weather vane, was the church in which Paul Revere was baptized and always attended.

Portrait of Cotton Mather (1663-1728) by Peter Pelham

Portrait of Judge Samuel Sewall (1688-1751) by John Smibert

**The Paul Revere House

Increase Mather, the second pastor of the North Church, lived in the parish house on North Square, later the site of the Paul Revere house. The original house is thought to have been destroyed in the fire of 1676. After it burned, John Jeffs built a house which was sold in 1681.

The Paul Revere House, end view, restored to the 17th century style

In the deed of that date he refers to it as "land with a dwelling." This charming seventeenth-century building is another example of the American interpretation of the medieval English or Tudor style of house, which the early settlers knew so well. It is to this style of architecture that the exterior was restored by Joseph E. Chandler in 1908. It is open to the public.

The original house was of the seventeenth-century colonial one-room plan with an end chimney, but it had two and one half stories instead of the typical one and a half. It was larger than many of the houses of that period

52

The Paul Revere House — of three stories, as it was when
he lived in it in the 18th century. Photographed by
W. A. French about 1880 before the restoration

with an unusual ell in the rear and an overhang not only
on the front but on the gable end as well. Both are finished
with pendent drops on the corners of the overhang. (See
illustration page 52.) The entrance door was of the early
American nail-studded type and the windows were diamond-paned casements. (See illustration page 41.)

This frame dwelling was almost one hundred years
old when Paul Revere bought it in 1770. It was then a
three-story house with sash windows and rectangular
panes, having been enlarged and changed so that it in no

53

way resembled the little house we see today. He needed a house of this size for his large family of sixteen children, although all did not live with him at one time. In 1800 he sold it and removed to Charter Street, not far away, where he died.

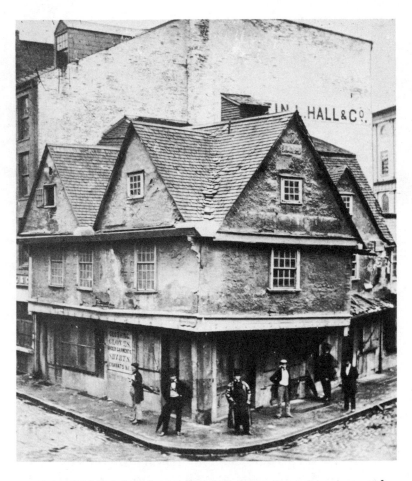

The Old Feather Store, Dock Square, from a stereograph of 1860

Other Famous Early American Buildings

The Old Feather Store, erected after the "terrible fire" of 1679 when seventy-seven houses and thirty-five warehouses burned, was a landmark until 1860. A picturesque gabled wooden frame building with a great chimney, it stood on the water front near Faneuil Hall in what is now Dock Square.

The First King's Chapel, built 1689, enlarged 1710, showing the wooden building and the beacon pole on Beacon Hill

The original King's Chapel, the first for Church of England worship, was erected in 1698 on the site of the present structure. This early wooden church had a spire with a crown and a cock weather vane.

At that time there were many wooden buildings nearby, including the first school, which stood on the present School Street. This was known as the Latin School or Free Writing School. It numbered among its students Benjamin Franklin and many other colonial boys who became prominent in later life.

The Beacon

The original beacon that gave the name to Beacon Hill was a tall pole mounted in 1634 on the top of Centry Hill (spelled Sentry later on) behind the present State House. (See illustration page 55.) It had a crane or arm sixty-five feet from the ground holding an iron bucket of tar which could be set afire to give warning in case of an enemy attack. A sentryman stood watch there but it was never necessary to use this beacon and it was not replaced after it was blown down.

Provincial Boston

When Boston became the capital of the Royal Province in 1692, the original Massachusetts Bay Colony Charter was vacated. The governors were no longer elected by the colonists here but were sent from England by royal ap-

The Old Province House, from a drawing originally owned by F. H. Manning

pointment. The Province House, a large mansion, was bought by the Province of Massachusetts in 1718 as a residence for these royal governors. It was one of the handsomest houses of the late seventeenth century in Boston — there were few others as elegant at the time.

Built by Peter Sergeant, a rich London merchant, it served as his residence until his death in 1714. Situated in the heart of the South End nearly opposite the end of Milk Street on Marlborough Street (now Washington Street) and across from the Old South Meetinghouse, this great house set well back from the "High Street" ("high" meaning fashionable). A grass lawn with two tall oak trees flanked the paved walk in front of the massive red stone entrance steps. These twenty steps were fitted with iron railings and led to a columned portico with a balcony on its roof. In the iron railing of this balcony was the date when the house was built, and the owner's initials: *16. P.S. 79.* A fence with porters' lodges at the ends and a central entrance gate separated the grounds from the highway. In the rear were the stables.

This three-story mansion, built of brick, was set upon a high basement. On the roof was a cupola surmounted by the famous Indian Archer weather vane made by Shem Drowne, the outstanding maker of weather vanes in the colonial period. This gilded bronze figure with glass eyes is now in the Massachusetts Historical Society's collection.

The luxurious interior of richly paneled spacious rooms was beautifully furnished and handsomely appointed with silk curtains and silver plate. The royal governors entertained elaborately. The ladies wore gorgeous hoopskirted gowns of French brocades or English Spitalfields silks and the gentlemen were elegant in embroidered waistcoats, knee breeches, and glittering swords. Many of the eighteenth-century colonial portraits on view at the Museum of Fine Arts reflect this splendor.

The Indian Archer Weathervane from the Old Province House by Shem Drowne

59

The Royal Arms were added to the front of the balcony when this mansion became the Province House. After the Declaration of Independence was read in Boston there was a feverish burning of all British insignia, but the panel with these arms was rescued and is now in the Massachusetts Historical Society.

For a while after the British left Boston, the Province House was used by Massachusetts government officials, but after the new State House was built in 1795 the old mansion deteriorated. Following a fire in 1864 it was torn down. However, some of the finest of the architectural details were saved, including the cedar paneling and the iron porch railing. These were incorporated in Indian Hill, a country house in West Newbury, Massachusetts, where they remained until a fire in 1959 destroyed all but one corner of the railing.

All this Tory splendor was in sharp contrast to the simplicity of most of colonial Boston, even in the eighteenth century. A traveler named Edward Ward writes in 1699: "The houses in some parts Joyn as in London — the Buildings, like their women being neat and handsome; their Streets, like the Hearts of the Male Inhabitants, are paved with Pebble. In the Chief High Street there are stately Edifaces some of which have cost the owners two or three thousand pounds the raising. . . . To the Glory of Religion and the Credit of the Town, there are four Churches."

Other Brick Houses

In 1693 the General Court passed an "Act for building of stone or brick in the Town of Boston preventing fire . . . henceforth no dwelling house, shop, warehouse, barn, stable or any other housing of more than eight feet in length or breadth and seven feet in height Shall be erected and set up in Boston but of stone or brick and covered with slate or tyle." This law was not enforced and wooden buildings continued to be built. However, as the eighteenth century progressed, many of the late colonial buildings were of brick and a few were of stone.

** The Moses Pierce-Hichborn House on Clark Square next to the Paul Revere house (now North Square) is one of these brick mansions. This house was built in 1711 on land originally owned by John Jeffs and later inherited by his daughter Mary, who sold it to her son, Moses, in 1710. At that time there were small shops on the property. In 1711 he removed the shops and built the three-story house of American brick with shallow arches above the sash windows still standing today and open to the public at certain times. Moses Pierce, one of the founders of the New North Church, was a glazier and his home was typical of the substantial residences built by the frugal and ambitious artisans of the times. These men had a certain social position although this is not always understood today.

This house also reflects the changes in colonial architecture and way of life that came in the eighteenth century. Gone is the old hall with its natural wood walls and

61

The Moses Pierce-Hichborn House, 1711, North Square

An interior view of the Hichborn House showing the staircase

diamond-paned casement windows. There are bed-chambers and other rooms now with sash windows and smaller fireplaces. However, the kitchen fireplace is large as it was in the seventeenth century.

Unlike most colonial houses, this house retains many original early eighteenth-century features of the interior as well as the exterior. Noteworthy among these is a fine American-Jacobean style staircase with turned balusters and pendent drops rarely found today.

The walls are plastered and the woodwork painted, some with a fine old red color. There are fireplace openings framed with their original bolection moulding (meaning a heavy wooden moulding around the fireplace opening), and some of the two-paneled doors with raised field panels are still here. This type of paneling was used on the walls and doors at this time and had the center of the panel raised and the edge beveled. The windows with their thick wooden mullions are also characteristic of the early eighteenth-century colonial style when the divisions between the rectangular glass panes of the sash windows were wider than in later windows. More "movables," or furnishings appeared now, and some splendid examples of these are on loan in these rooms.

In the 1770's, a few years after his cousin Paul Revere bought the house next door, this house was sold to Nathaniel Hichborn, a boatbuilder, hence its present name.

On Union Street, which was laid out in 1636, is the ** Capen House, the early eighteenth century brick home of Hopestill Capen, sergeant in the Ancient and Honor-

The Capen House, built about 1714

able Artillery. This three-story town house still has its original slate roof and old brick façade with three shallow arches above the windows on the second floor. It also has the usual string-courses or projecting horizontal bands of bricks, between the rows of windows, which became so characteristic of colonial brick houses, giving them the name "belted houses."

65

This house, probably built before 1714, was bought by Thomas Stoddard in 1742. Later his daughter Patience and her husband, Hopestill Capen, inherited it. Here at the "Sign of the Cornfields" he ran his dry-goods store.

In 1769 one of Hopestill's apprentices was Benjamin Thompson of Woburn, who became a distinguished sci-

Birthplace of Count Rumford, Woburn — 1714

entist. He lived abroad after the Revolutionary War and returned as Count Rumford. He was a great benefactor of science and left legacies to both the Academy of Arts and Sciences and Harvard College. The Rumford Professorship at Harvard was established in his honor.

66

Later Isaiah Thomas published his newspaper the *Massachusetts Spy* here from 1771 to 1775. This pro-liberty publication was hurriedly moved to Worcester when it became too dangerous to print it in Boston and there became the *Worcester Spy*.

The Duc de Chartres, afterward King Louis Philippe, when in exile was a guest in this house and he gave French lessons here while awaiting funds from abroad.

Hopestill Capen died in 1807 and the house was inherited by his son, Thomas Capen, who was also a shopkeeper here until his death in 1819. At that time the house was assessed for $5,000.

In 1826 the oyster business came to the Capen house and is still being carried on here as the Olde Oyster House. This fascinating old restaurant now occupies the adjoining old brick house (two windows wide) as well as the Capen house, and the original oyster bar is still in use.

Nearby is the Ebenezer Hancock house on Marshall's Lane, built about 1760. John Hancock inherited it from his uncle Thomas in 1764. This splendid brick house is a typical town house of a gentleman of the period. It has the usual three stories, shallow arches over sash windows with rectangular panes, and brick string-courses. Inside, there still remains some good colonial paneling upstairs.

Ebenezer was John Hancock's younger brother. He occupied this house as a combination office and residence in 1776 when he was deputy paymaster and here he gave out the back pay to the Continental troops in 1778. This urgently needed money came from France as a result of Benjamin Franklin's negotiations.

67

In 1789 this house became the property of Ebenezer Frothingham, a merchant who had his china and glass shop on the ground floor. Later that year Benjamin Fuller kept his shop there. In 1821 William H. Learnard opened his store in this building, selling "Boots, Shoes and Rubbers,"

The oldest shoe store in Boston

continuing in business until his death in 1886. This shop remains in business today as Leonard and Company, 10 Marshall Street, and is carried on in the old manner by Mr. George H. Tarbox. It is the oldest shoe store in Boston.

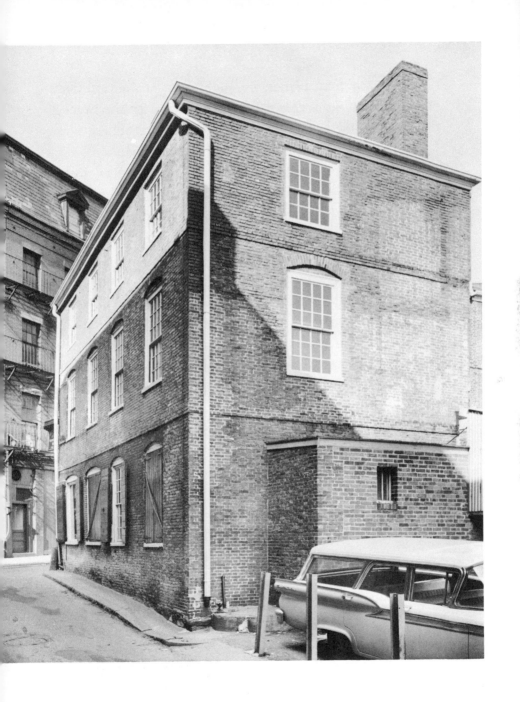

The Ebenezer Hancock House

In 1764 John Hancock bought most of the land close by on Creek Square, and later, "shortly after the peace," he built a block of brick town houses there. These were joined together and known as Hancock Row.

At the corner of Hanover and Union streets, Josiah Franklin, father of the famous Benjamin, had his home and shop in 1712. He had been a dyer in England but in Boston he set up a business of chandlery and soap boiling. His shop sign was a ** blue ball hanging from an iron bracket attached to the wall of the house. This sign may still be seen at the Old State House in the Bostonian Society Collection. The parlor and dining room were close behind his shop and there were many visitors who came seeking his sound advice on town and church matters. There were also many children, as there were in most families of those days, and Benjamin notes in his *Autobiography* that "thirteen sitting at one time at his father's table all grew up to be men and women and married."

The Blue Ball — Shop sign of Benjamin Franklin's father

70

The Green Dragon Tavern, Union Street, where the
Boston Tea Party was planned

Taverns

Not far away on historic Union Street was the celebrated Green Dragon Tavern, a two-and-a-half-story
brick building where the leading patriots met. Daniel
Webster called the Green Dragon the headquarters of the
Revolution. Many plans were laid here, including those
for the Boston Tea Party. This wonderful old Boston
tavern was built in 1680, and stood until 1828. The site
is now marked with a ** plaque on a building at 84 Union
Street.

Another famous tavern was the Bunch of Grapes in King's Street, built as early as 1712 in the South End at what is now the corner of Kilby and State streets. It was the meeting place of the Grand Lodge of Masons founded in 1733 with Paul Revere as the first master. It was also in front of this tavern that all the British emblems and ornaments that could be found, such as the lion and the unicorn on the State House, were burned in a bonfire after the reading of the Declaration of Independence. Washington and his officers dined here and Lafayette came in 1784. The Society of the Cincinnati also met at this tavern in 1787.

These taverns were the news centers of the town until newspapers were printed. The first newspaper in the country was the *Boston News Letter* of 1704. In 1719 the *Boston Gazette* was published weekly, followed by the *New England Courant* which was published by Benjamin Franklin's older brother James.

One of the oldest standing brick buildings in Boston is the original home of the ** Old Corner Book Store at the corner of Washington and School streets. On this historic site stood the home of Anne Hutchinson before she was banished from the colony in 1634 for her views on religion.

The present brick building was erected by Thomas Cresse in 1712, after the great fire, and served as his home and apothecary shop, the first in Boston. Later it housed a publishing house, the *Atlantic Monthly*, and after that the famous bookstore which still continues in business nearby.

This original eighteenth century brick building, now

THE
New-England Courant.

From MONDAY February 4. to MONDAY February 11. 1723.

The late Publisher of this Paper, finding so many Inconveniences would arise by his carrying the Manuscripts and publick News to be supervis'd by the Secretary, as to render his carrying it on unprofitable, has intirely dropt the Undertaking. The present Publisher having re.civ'd the following Piece, desires the Readers to accept of it as a Preface to what they may hereafter meet with in this Paper.

Non ego mordaci distrinxi Carmine quenquam,
Nulla venenato Litera mista Joco est.

LONG has the Press groaned in bringing forth an hateful, but numerous Brood of Party Pamphlets, malicious Scribbles, and Billingsgate Ribaldry. The Rancour and bitterness it has unhappily infused into Mens minds, and to what a Degree it has sowred and leaven'd the Tempers of Persons formerly esteemed some of the most sweet and affable, is too well known here, to need eny further Proof or Representation of the Matter.

No generous and impartial Person then can blame the present Undertaking, which is designed purely for the Diversion and Merriment of the Reader. Pieces of Pleasancy and Mirth have a secret Charm in them to allay the Heats and Tumours of our Spirits, and to make a Man forget his restless Resentments. They have a strange Power to tune the harsh Disorders of the Soul, and reduce us to a serene and placid State of Mind.

The main Design of this Weekly Paper will be to entertain the Town with the most comical and diverting Incidents of Humane Life, which in so large a Place as *Boston*, will not fail of a universal Exemplification : Nor shall we be wanting to fill up these Papers with a grateful Interspersion of more serious Morals, which may be drawn from the most ludicrous and odd Parts of Life.

As for the Author, that is the next Question. But tho' we profess our selves ready to oblige the ingenious and courteous Reader with most Sorts of Intelligence, yet here we beg a Reserve. Nor will it be of any Manner of Advantage either to them or to the Writers, that their names should be published ; and therefore in this Matter we desire the Favour of you to suffer us to hold our Tongues : Which tho' at this Time of Day it may sound like a very uncommon Request, yet it proceeds from the very Hearts of your Humble Servants.

By this Time the Reader perceives that more than one are engaged in the present Undertaking. Yet is there one Person, an Inhabitant of this Town of *Boston*, whom we honour as a Doctor in the Chair, or a perpetual Dictator.

The Society had design'd to present the Publick with his Effigies, but that the Limner, to whom he was presented for a Draught of his Countenance, descryed (and this he is ready to offer upon Oath) Nineteen Features in his Face, more than ever he beheld in any Humane Visage before ; which so raised the Price of his Picture, that our Master himself forbid the Extravagance of coming up to it. And then besides, the Limner objected a Schi m in his face, which spits it from his Forehead in a strait Line down to his Chin, in such sort, that Mr. Painter protests it is a double Face, and he'll have

Four Pounds foa the Pourtraiture. However, tho' this double Face has spoilt us of a pretty Picture, yet we all rejoiced to see old *Janus* in our Company.

There is no Man in *Boston* better qualified than old *Janus* for a *Couranteer*, or if you please, an *Observator*, being a Man of such remarkable *Opticks*, as to look two ways at once.

As for his Morals, he is a chearly Christian, as the Country Phrase expresses it. A Man of good Temper, courteous Deportment, sound Judgment ; a mortal Hater of Nonsense, Foppery, Formality, and endless Ceremony.

As for his Club, they aim at no greater Happiness or Honour, than the Publick be made to know, that it is the utmost of their Ambition to attend upon and do all imaginable good Offices to good Old *Janus* the Couranteer, who is and always will be the Readers humble Servant.

P. S. Gentle Readers, we design never to let a Paper pass without a Latin Motto if we can possibly pick one up, which carries a Charm in it to the Vulgar, and the learned admire the pleasure of Construing. We should have obliged the World with a Greek scrap or two, but the Printer has no Types, and therefore we intreat the candid Reader not to impute the defect to our Ignorance, for our Doctor can say all the *Greek* Letters by heart.

His Majesty's Speech to the Parliament, October 11.
tho' already publish'd, may perhaps be new to many of
our Country Readers ; we shall therefore insert it in this
Day's Paper.

His MAJESTY's most Gracious SPEECH to both Houses of Parliament, on Thursday October 11. 1722.

My Lords and Gentlemen,

I Am sorry to find my self obliged, at the Opening of this Parliament, to acquaint you, That a dangerous Conspiracy has for some time formed, and is still carrying on against my Person and Government, in Favour of a Popish Pretender.

The Discoveries I have made here, the Informations I have received from my Ministers abroad, and the Intelligences I have had from the Powers in Alliance with me, and indeed from most parts of Europe, have given me most ample and current Proofs of this wicked Design.

The Conspirators have, by their Emissaries, made the strongest Instances for Assistance from Foreign Powers, but were disappointed in their Expectations : However, confiding in their Numbers, and not discouraged by their former ill Success, they resolved (once more, upon their own strength, to attempt the subversion of my Government.

To this end they provided considerable Sums of Money, engaged great Numbers of Officers from abroad, secured large Quantities of Arms and Ammunition, and thought themselves in such Readiness, that had not the Conspiracy been timely discovered, we should, without doubt, before now have seen the whole Nation, and particularly the City of London, involved in Blood and Confusion.

The Care I have taken has, by the Blessing of God, hitherto prevented the Execution of their trayterous Projects. The Troops have been incamped all this Summer ; six Regiments (though very necessary for the Security of that Kingdom) have been brought over from *Ireland* ; The States General have given me assurances that they would keep a considerable Body of Forces in readiness to embark on the first Notice of their being wanted here ; which was all I desired

The Old Corner Bookstore, built about 1712

disgraced and almost concealed by trade signs, is under-
neath a fine example of our colonial architecture and an
important landmark. It seems a pity that the buildings still
standing in Boston like this one cannot be restored to their
former dignity.

74

Boston was growing rapidly, and in 1722 Captain John Bonner drew his excellent map of the town. (See pages 6, 7.) This, and Price's Map of 1767, are reprinted and on sale today. Both are well worth studying in order to understand and enjoy colonial Boston.

Other Colonial Brick Buildings

Beautiful red-brick churches, public buildings, and homes were erected in the early eighteenth century in Boston. Many of these remain cherished for their historic significance and for their fine colonial architecture. They were an American interpretation of the English early Georgian style, simplified but distinguished.

Outstanding among them is historic ** Christ Church on Salem Street in the North End, now called the "Old North Church." This second Episcopal Church in Boston was built in 1723 by James Varney and Ebenezer Clough, masons. The architect is unknown but is thought to have been William Price who designed the spire.

The plain colonial exterior is of American bricks which were made in Medford. The beautiful high steeple dominated the area. It was built with funds contributed by Honduras merchants and served as a landmark guiding vessels into the harbor. It shows clearly on the harbor charts of 1740 and in the early engravings of the shoreline of Boston including a notable one of 1768 by William Price.

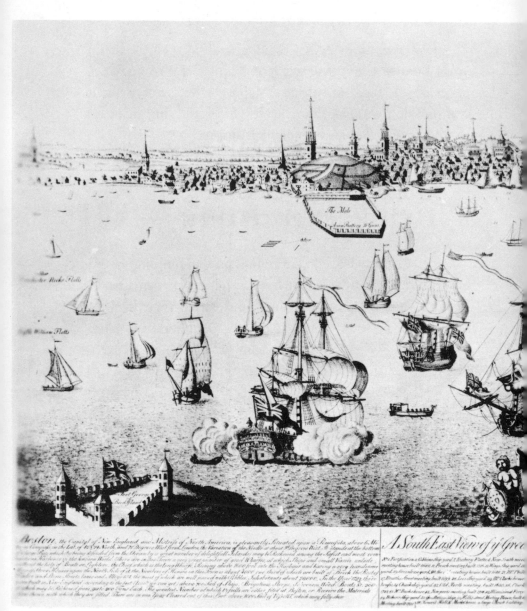

Southeast view of Boston by William Price, 17

...owing the ships and church steeples

In 1804 it was blown down by a hurricane and a new one was erected by Joseph Tucker in 1807 from a design by Charles Bulfinch. Another hurricane in 1954 destroyed this steeple. The present restoration is a copy of the first or colonial spire and is surmounted by the original weather vane. This was made by Shem Drowne in 1740 in the form of a banner with a ball and a star above. The belfry was made famous by Henry Wadsworth Longfellow's poem *Paul Revere's Ride*. Here the lantern signals according to tradition are thought to have been hung on the evening of April 18, 1775, warning of the movements of the British.

In the tower are the eight original bells that were used in colonial days to toll the curfew and for other occasions, and are still often rung today. They were made in Gloucester, England, by Abel Rudhall and hung in 1744. Each has a different inscription and some have the initials of the maker *A.R.* Number three is marked *"We are the first ring cast for the British Empire in North America A. R. 1744."* Number five is marked *"William Shirley, Esq. Governor of Massachusetts Bay in New England, anno 1744"* and was given by him. Paul Revere as a boy was one of the bellringers.

The windows are the originals, arched sash style with rectangular panes of clear white glass.

The interior, which seats more than five hundred, was restored in 1912 and has the colonial style box pews with paneled doors and narrow wooden board seats. Among the pew owners was Paul Revere's son, Joseph Warren Revere, who attended this church and bought pew number 54 in 1808. The "Bay Pew" was reserved for

78

*Exterior of Christ Church, Salem Street. Old photograph
taken from Hull Street*

Interior of Christ Church, now called the "Old North Church,"
showing the box pews and the chandeliers

the use of "The Gentlemen of the Bay of Honduras," being set apart in 1727 for these merchants who gave the steeple.

The galleries are along the sides and the organ loft is at the opposite end from the altar as was usual in colonial

Interior of Christ Church showing the organ loft

churches of this time. The carved figures of trumpeting angels were given to the church in 1746 and were said to have been taken from a French privateer when she was captured on her way to Canada. The clock on the face of the organ-loft gallery, installed in 1726, was made by Richard Avery.

81

The colonial-style high pulpit with its ascending steps and sounding board suspended above is a restoration, and the large arched window above the altar table is now re-opened.

The original painter's bills record a rich color treatment in the interior, not as we see it today. There was to be "cedar graining on the gallery faces and the wrought-iron chandelier supports were to be Prussian blue picked out with vermilion red. The carving was to be picked out in gold and the ceiling whitewashed."

The Communion plate and the "Vinegar Bible" were presented in 1733 by King George II of England. This Bible was called "Vinegar" because of an error in the printing of 1719 in a chapter of Saint Luke which should have read "Vineyard" but was printed "Vinegar" in these editions.

Under the church are tomb vaults. One was identified in 1812 as that of a Mr. Thomas who was buried here about ten years after the church was built. There are legends about others, including Major Pitcairn, but the identities of those who lie here and the number of tombs are still a mystery.

This colonial church is the oldest now standing in Boston and the only one which has had one form of worship and continuous services except for the period when it was closed by the British from 1775 to 1783. It is open to the public daily.

** The Old South Meetinghouse on Washington Street at the corner of Milk Street is another red-brick colonial church of historic interest. Built in 1729, to re-

*Exterior of the Old South Meeting house, built 1729,
replacing an earlier wooden meeting house*

*The Harris Pitcher by Ebenezer Moulton, 1810, showing the
Old South Meeting house on fire*

place an earlier wooden meetinghouse of 1669 which stood on the same site, it is an important landmark today. This area was originally part of Governor Winthrop's garden.

In the first building Benjamin Franklin was baptized in 1706. The present building with its original graceful spire of wood was built of American brick. The architect was Robert Twelves and the cornerstone bears the initials of Joshua Blanchard, a well-known mason of his day. The design follows the usual colonial pattern with the belfry and a spire above rising from a porch on the entrance façade. The tower clock, made by Gawen Brown, was added to this third Congregational Church about 1770. Later, when the neighborhood became commercial and the parishioners had moved away, the congregation transferred to a new residential district. The original bell was hung in the new Old South Church building in Copley Square in 1877 and still peals from this newer tower.

The interior suffered at the hands of the British soldiers during the Revolutionary War. All the old boxed pews, save one, were ripped out and burned for firewood. The beautiful carved pew with silken hangings belonging to Deacon Hubbard was taken out and used as a pigsty. The south door was closed and a leaping bar for horses installed. The east gallery was reserved for spectators and a refreshment bar was placed in the other gallery. Hundreds of cartloads of dirt were dumped on the floor to create a riding ring, and here the Queen's Light Dragoons were trained.

The original elevated pulpit was torn out and many valuable books and manuscripts stored in the tower room were burned. One of these was miraculously saved and turned up in England many years later. Fortunately this priceless volume, *Bradford's History Of The Plimoth Plantation,* came back to Boston in 1897, and is now in the State House. This meetinghouse was restored for worship in 1782.

Boston continued to be plagued by fires, not only by the "great fires" but by others as well. In 1810 this meetinghouse was almost lost when the roof caught on fire. Isaac Harris, a mast maker, climbed to the roof and helped to put out the flames with so much courage that he later received a silver pitcher in recognition of his bravery. ** This pitcher, made by Ebenezer Moulton, and inscribed "For his intrepid and successful exhertions on the roof of the Old South Church when on Fire Dec. 29nth 1810," may be seen at the Museum of Fine Arts.

In 1876 the Old South Church was again threatened with destruction, this time to make way for business and office buildings. A Society of Ladies, organized for the purpose, together with other citizens, protested and raised funds totaling $400,000 to save it. This historic shrine deserves to be more completely restored and appreciated today. It is open to the public daily.

As Boston grew there was need for a new market and a hall for town meetings. Peter Faneuil (pronounced Fanel or Funel) recognized this need. Born in New Rochelle, New York, in 1700, the son of a French Huguenot refugee, he was the oldest of eleven children. Following his father's death, he came to Boston at the age of eighteen, to be with his uncle Andrew Faneuil. Here he engaged in

86

business and acquired some property but it was not until 1737, after the death of Andrew Faneuil, a rich merchant who left him his fortune, that he became the wealthiest Bostonian of his day. In 1740 he offered to the town the

The original Faneuil Hall, 1742

necessary funds to construct this building. Although his generous gift was accepted by a majority of only seven votes, the beautiful ** Faneuil Hall was erected in 1742. It stood on the water front of the Town Cove, now Dock Square.

87

John Smibert, the early colonial portrait painter, was the architect-designer and Samuel Ruggles the builder.

This red-brick building, much smaller than it is today, was forty feet wide by one hundred feet long and two and a half stories high. There were nine open arches on the ground floor for the stalls and shops of the market and nine arched windows above in the hall. There were pilasters

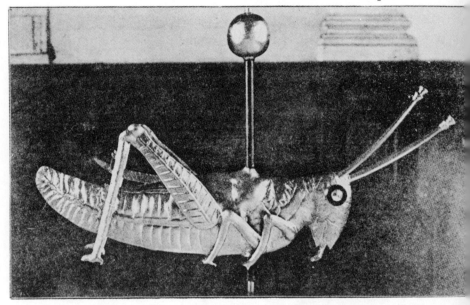

*The Grasshopper Weathervane on Faneuil Hall by
Shem Drowne*

on the façade between the windows and the roof was crowned with dormer windows. The square tower ended in a domed cupola with a weather vane in the form of a grasshopper, a symbol of trade.

In 1805 Charles Bulfinch, the outstanding architect of that time, enlarged and rebuilt the old Faneuil Hall into the splendid building we see today. He added a third story, as there was need for more space, but he replaced the cupola and the original colonial grasshopper weather vane.

This weather vane with glass eyes was made by Shem Drowne and was probably inspired by a similar grasshopper on the Royal Exchange in London. Thrown down by an earthquake in 1755 and a fire in 1761, it was put up again in 1763 and stayed in place until it was repaired and replaced in 1862. There it can be seen today.

The ground floor has been in continuous use as a market for about two hundred years. Above is the hall made famous by colonial orators with their passionate appeals for liberty. In a speech delivered here in 1763 this historic meeting place was called by James Otis "The Cradle of Liberty."

For many years the largest hall in Boston, it was used for the most important social as well as political events. In 1744 soon after its completion there was a "Concert of Music" presented to celebrate the Coronation Day of George II of England.

By vote of the town, Faneuil Hall was illuminated when the Stamp Act was repealed in 1766. During the Revolutionary War the British soldiers gave plays there. Many important banquets and receptions have been held in this famous old room, including one for Lafayette in 1784 and Washington in 1789. In 1833 powerful appeals for anti-slavery echoed from its walls. Still in use today, it is never rented but is "forever free." Open weekdays 9-5, Saturday 9-12.

On the third floor above are the Headquarters and Museum (both open without charge) of the Ancient and

Honorable Artillery Company, which was founded in 1637 and is the oldest military company in the United States. Open Monday through Friday 10-4.

Peter Faneuil lived to see the completion of the original building although he died soon after at the age of forty-two. He was a bachelor who lived well and spent freely but wisely. From his letters we learn that he ordered the "very best Madeira wine . . . for the use of my house . . . but not of the strongest sort." "The latest best book of the several sorts of cookery, which pray let be of the largest character, for the benefit of the maid's reading," and "a handsome chariot with two sets of harness, with the arms, as enclosed, on the same, in the handsomest manner that you shall judge proper, but at the same time nothing gaudy." He also owned slaves, English horses, other buildings, and vessels.

His fine house, formerly his uncle's, stood opposite the King's Chapel on what is now Tremont Street. Set back from the highway in terraced gardens, this large stone mansion was of three stories with four chimneys and a hip roof finished with a roof rail at the top. There were long windows with keystoned lintels of stone above, pilasters at the ends of the façade, and a balcony over the entrance door. It was a great American Georgian house. Here he entertained lavishly, as the quotations above indicate.

The furnishings of his home were elaborate even for the eighteenth century in Boston and his inventory of them is a revealing colonial document. This may be seen in the Suffolk County Probate Office in the Court House.

Portrait of Peter Faneuil by John Smibert

Inventory of the Estate of the late Peter Faneuil Esq. deceased) taken & appraised by us the Subscribers the 28 March 1743.

Viz.

Item	£	
12 Carved Veneerd Chairs & a Couch	105	
a Large Pier Glass	110	
Arms to ditto	7.10	
1 Chimney Glass & Arms	35	
1 Marble Table	20	
1 Large Turkey Carpet	35	
1 Compleat Brass hearth, dogs Tongs Shovells Bellows &c	18	
1 Copper Tea Table, 8 Cupps, Saucers, Tea Pott, Stand Bowl, & Sugar Dish	10	
3 Alablaster Bowls & Stands	6	
a parcell China, Delph Glasses, of Severall Sorts	199	515.10
1. 8 Day Walnutt Case Clock	10	
1 Marble Table	15	
12 plain Walnutt Frame Leather Bottom Chairs	21	
1 Chimney Glass	12	
1 Mohogony Table	6	
1 Glass Sconce and a pr Arms	3.10	
7 Small ditto with Arms	7	
4 Mezitinto pieces & 1 Other Sort	5	
Prospect of Boston	10	
2 Land skips on Copper	3	
Temple of Solomon	10	
1 pr Andirons, Tongs, Shovell of Steel, & a pr Bellows	10	128.10
1 Large Ovall Mohogony Table	10	
1 Marble Table	12	
1 Large Entry Lanthorn	12	
12 Baggs & Bucketts	15	
150 Pictures	75	
97. ditto with Glasses	19.8	
Alexander's Battles	10	
Erasmus	2.10	155.18
1 Pier Glass	30	
1 Dressing Glass and Draws	10	
12 Chairs & a Couch	56	
1 Chimney Glass	12	
Carried Over	£ 103	329.18

Item	Value	Total
97 ditto with Glafses	19.8	
Alexander's Battles	10	
Erasmus	2.10	155.18
1 Pier Glafs	30	
1 Drefsing Glafs and Draws	10	
12 Chairs & a couch	56	
1 Chimney Glafs	12	108
1 Green Harrateen Bed, Bedstead, Window Curtains, Cushions, Mattrafs, 2 green Silk Quilt, feather Bed	65	
3 Sconces with Arms	3	
1 Burreau Table	10	
1 pair Brafs Faced Dogs, Fire Shovell Tongs & Bellows	4	
1 Turkey-workt Carpet	25	
1 Silver hilted Sword, pair pistols & powder flask	15	
1 case with 6 Razors, pair Sisors bone Penknive, strap, 2 Bottles, Looking Glafs Tipt with Silver	15	
1 Case with 6 Razors, hone & Strap Ordinary	5	250
Yellow Mohair Bed Counterpain feather Bed, Bolster 2 Pillows false curtains & with 6 chairs, a great chair, 2 Stools, — Window Curtains & cushion all of the same for	180	
1 Brafs hearth, Andirons, Shovell, Tongs & Bellows	12	
1 Desk and Book Case with Glafses	40	
1 Chimney Glafs and a pair Sconces	15	
1 Second Glafs and Drefsing Table	6.10	
6 Lignumvitia Chocolate cupps Lined with Silver	3	
1 curious white & Blew Teapott	1.10	
1 Large Turkey workt Carpet	25	
1 Small Ditto	4	237
6 Cain & Two arm chairs	16	
1 Chimney Glafs	10	
1 Sconce with Arms 20L 1 Chamber Table 3L	23	
1 Dutch Prefs	10	
1 English Walnutt Desk	10	
1 Workt Bed, Bolsters, Pillows 3/4 Lined with Green Damask Mohogny Bedstead Blew Silk Quilt	110	

First page of Peter Faneuil's Household Inventory, 1743

By this time Boston had come a long way from the rugged existence and simple life of the seventeenth century. Although there were few merchants as well off as Peter Faneuil, life in the eighteenth century was dignified, gracious, and often luxurious. The colonial portraits record for us the rich clothes and fine furnishings of these ladies and gentlemen at the end of this era of pre-Revolutionary Boston.

---

1 pair Brafs Faced Andirons, Tongs & Shovell	5	
1 Chints Field Mohogony Bedstead Feather Bed Bolster Pillow & Ruggs	30	
1 Small green Screen	1.10	
China Window Curtains	3	
1 pair Large Dogs	6	
1 Carpet	1.10	
1 Marble Table	12	238
1 Blew Harateen Bed Bolsters Pillows, Silk Quilt Window curtains, Squab & Mahogony Bedstead	40	
1 Turkey workt carpet	25	
1 Old couch	3	
1 Carpet	15	
1 Square Table	3	
24 Cain Chairs	48	
1 Cloth Drefs	5	
1 Sconce	3.10	
1 Ovall Table	3	
1 Silk purple Quilt	10	
224 Copper Potts, Pans, Brafs Kettles & 350 Pewter	181.16	
1 Large Copper Trevit	30	
1 Brafs Kettle about 10 gallon	5	
1 pair Large Tongs Andirons & Shovells	3	
3 Andirons	3.10	
2 Frying Panns	3	

94

Detail of the Old State House, the English Lion and the Unicorn

The Old State House

** The Old State House, or first colonial Town House of brick, was erected in 1712 on the site of the earlier wooden Town House which had burned, along with many other buildings in the neighborhood, in the fire of 1711.

Situated at the head of King's Street, now State Street, this splendid building looked down the principal street to Long Wharf, built in 1710, and the harbor. Here the ships from England tied up and the royal governors marched up King's Street to the State House to be received. Proclamations such as the *Repeal of the Stamp Act* and the *Declaration of Independence* were read from the balcony to crowds of colonists in the wide street below. Later the Boston Massacre took place here, one of the incendiary events leading to the Revolutionary War.

This most beautiful of our colonial buildings in Boston was rebuilt in 1748. The architect is unknown but the building reflects the contemporary English-Georgian style and is more richly ornamented than most of the colonial buildings. The exterior was embellished with carved wooden details and British emblems, such as the lion and the unicorn which adorned the east gable, and a sundial set in the wall between them. Below was the famous balcony and above this a handsome pedimented window. Today, the exterior stands more as it was originally than any of the early public buildings, with the exception of a subway entrance which defaces the ground floor.

In spite of a terrible fire in 1747, which destroyed the interior and many valuable paintings, furnishings, books, and records, the exterior walls remained. When the interior was rebuilt, it was used mostly for the Massachusetts Legislature and the courts.

In 1768 it served as a barracks for the British troops. After the Revolution it was used as a State House until the larger one was built on Beacon Street by Charles Bulfinch in 1795. In 1828 it housed the United States Post Office with fifteen employees. Later it was rented by the

Exterior of the Old State House

city to mercantile establishments and was defaced by their signs and a Mansart (spelled Mansard in America) roof. In 1882 the exterior was restored to its present appearance by George A. Clough. It is still owned by the city.

The Bostonian Society prevented the destruction of the Old State House and has maintained their splendid Museum and Library there, open free to the public. This collection contains outstanding material related to the history of Boston.

Independence

Three buildings in Boston, Faneuil Hall, the Old South Meetinghouse, and the Old State House were more closely connected with the birth of our independence than any others in the country, excepting Independence Hall in Philadelphia. Meetings led by our great patriots to plan resistance against tyranny were held frequently in these colonial brick structures.

Town meetings were first held in the Town House, as the Old State House was then called. After Faneuil Hall was built, the colonists met there in the larger hall and that became "The Cradle of Liberty." In 1761 when this hall was not large enough to hold all the enraged colonists they moved over to the Old South Meetinghouse and it was at one of these "body meetings," so called, that they organized for the Boston Tea Party.

All three buildings are standing today on their original sites, great symbols of American freedom.

98

Exterior of King's Chapel, the stone building erected in 1749

King's Chapel

** In 1749 the first King's Chapel, a wooden building built in 1688, was replaced by the present stone church at the corner of Tremont and School streets. The cornerstone was laid by Governor Shirley. Peter Harrison, a gentleman-architect-designer of Newport, Rhode Island, drew up the plans. Among other details they included a balustrade and a graceful spire which for lack of funds were never completed. Even the portico was not built in the colonial period. When George Washington was in Boston in 1789 he attended a concert in his honor here, on Christmas night, and contributed to the fund then being raised for this portico of wooden columns which was finished the next year.

The bell cracked during an evening service in 1814 and was replaced in 1816 by a new one cast by Paul Revere. This bell, made at the Revere Foundry in Canton, Massachusetts, was the heaviest ever cast there, weighing 2,475 pounds. It was made of the metal from the original bell with more added. Paul Revere, the patriot and silversmith, also cast 398 other bells and this one was number 161. It is still ringing from King's Chapel today.

There were very few stone buildings in colonial Boston as there was little stone available. The granite for this important church came from Quincy. It was taken from the surface of the ground, as no quarries had been opened at the time, and brought to Boston by water.

Interior of King's Chapel, the organ loft

The interior of King's Chapel is like a bit of old London with its stone floor, burial vaults below and beautiful eighteenth century epitaphs, memorials, and effigies in marble and bronze.

Although the architectural details of this second King's Chapel building follow the usual colonial plan, they are richer. The galleries at the sides are accented with eight beautiful coupled Corinthian columns. There is a Palladian window (a group of three with the center one

Interior of King's Chapel, the box pews, columns and pulpit

arched) high on the wall above the altar table. On the opposite wall, over the entrance door, is the organ loft where
a clock by Ebenezer Oliver is set in the gallery face.

The pulpit dates from 1717 and is in the usual early
eighteenth century style. Paneled and pilastered, it is ap-
proached by a balustraded stair and has a sounding board
suspended above it.

In the center and at the sides are box pews enclosed by doors and on the right side is a larger one. This pew, for the use of the royal governor, was removed after the Revolution, but it was later restored with its canopy and red silk hangings. Pew number 20 was owned by Sir Charles Henry Frankland, who, with Governor Shirley and Peter Faneuil, was a generous contributor to this church.

Interior of King's Chapel, the colonial governor's pew restored

The original organ, purchased in England in 1756, for this stone building, was also used for concerts. It was one of the few in Boston because at this time music was considered inappropriate to worship in the meetinghouses other than those of the Church of England.

The custom of decorating the church with sweet-smelling greens at Christmas time was also observed only in these churches.

Many of the treasures of King's Chapel were gifts to the original wooden church. Among these are the panels on the chancel wall above the communion table which were presented by King William III of England. These are of black lettered in gold.

The rare leather-bound books sent for the chapel in 1698 by King William III are now in the Boston Athenaeum.

A set of red cushions and vestments was given by Queen Anne and during her reign (1702 to 1714) this church was known as the Queen's Chapel.

The church plate, according to Francis Hill Bigelow in his book *Historic Silver of the Colonies and Its Makers,* has disappeared. "This silver was carried off by Dr. Henry Caner, the last royalist rector of this church. To be sure it was largely the work of English goldsmiths and the gifts of the British sovereigns, William and Mary, George II and George III, but doubtless there were also pieces made by colonial silversmiths. The pieces known to have been taken by Dr. Caner to Canada consisted of six flagons, six cups, four large basins, six dishes, two christening basins, six salvers, and four tankards, etc." There is also some church silver in the Museum of Fine Arts said to be "*William and Mary's gift to their Majesty's chapel in New England, King's Chapel, which gave them to Christ Church, Cambridge.*" The present communion plate dates from after the Revolution and includes a graceful silver ewer made by Paul Revere in 1798.

This first Episcopal Church in New England became the first Unitarian Church in the country. Both the First Church of Boston and King's Chapel are today Unitarian churches. They are open to the public.

Other Burial Grounds

** The Old South Burying Ground was laid out in 1660. Later it was called the Old Granary Burial Ground as it was beside the old Town Granary, a long wooden building used for storing the colonists' grain. There are more than sixteen hundred graves with a wide variety of stones and monuments. Among the well-known colonial people buried here are: Judge Samuel Sewall, Peter Faneuil or Funel as his table-style stone is marked, Benjamin Franklin's parents to whom a cenotaph was erected in the nineteenth century, and Paul Revere, patriot and silversmith. Here also in this old cemetery on Tremont Street are the graves of the victims of the Boston Massacre, several governors including Christopher Gore and John Hancock, and three signers of the *Declaration of Independence*, James Otis, Samuel Adams, and Robert Treat Paine.

The Old Granary Burying Ground, the oldest stones and tombs

The Central Burying Ground — on the Common, old stones and wall tombs.

** The Central Burying Ground was laid out in the southwest corner of the Common in 1756. Although it was the last of the four colonial graveyards it has many interesting stones and wall tombs. Here were buried British soldiers who died during the Revolutionary War and later, Julien, the famous cook, who invented the soup which bears his name.

Here, too, Gilbert Stuart, the portrait painter, was buried. Born in Narragansett, Rhode Island, in 1775, the

Gilbert Stuart plaque

son of a snuff grinder, he later traveled abroad and painted extensively. He came to live permanently in Boston in 1806 and resided on Essex Street. Outstanding among his American portraits is the head of George Washington whom he painted from life in 1796. ** This portrait, known as "The Athenaeum Head," is on loan from the Boston Athenaeum to the ** Museum of Fine Arts, Boston and hangs in the Museum with the companion portrait of Martha Washington.

*Portrait of John Hancock (1737-1815) by
John Singleton Copley*

Colonial Houses
on Beacon Street

Across the Common on that part of Beacon Hill
which is now Beacon Street lived another great American
portrait painter, John Singleton Copley. Here his home *
(now marked by a plaque on the site) was a two-story
colonial house on a large town farm. He painted the portraits, so well known today, of colonial ladies and gentlemen dressed in their best attire.

108

*Portrait of Mercy Otis Warren (1728-1814) by
John Singleton Copley*

When he was a boy, after his Irish father died, he helped his mother keep a tobacco shop on Long Wharf. Later she married Peter Pelham, who taught her son so much about painting. Young Copley worked long hours and prospered but was restless and extravagant. His portrait of Paul Revere was probably painted to discharge a debt to his friend for making silver and gold frames for miniatures. Later Copley went to England never to return. Many of his portraits, including ** those of Paul Revere and John Hancock, may be seen at the Museum of Fine Arts.

Higher up on Beacon Street stood the * Hancock House on another town farm. This stately house was built in 1737 by Thomas Hancock and was inherited by his nephew John Hancock.

This two-and-a-half-story mansion was of stone with a gambrel roof, four chimneys, dormer windows, and a roof rail at the top. There were stone quoins or blocks on the corners and around the windows. This Connecticut stone was brought to Boston by boat. The house was set high and a little back from the street with a paved walk leading to a flight of stone entrance steps. At the side were gardens with flower beds bordered with box leading to a summerhouse. There were also box trees of great height, a variety of fruit trees, and several large mulberry trees. Behind the house were the stable, coach house, and pastures for the cows and horses.

The interior was sumptuous as Miss Eliza G. Gardner, who lived there several years describes it: "As you enter the governor's mansion, to the right was the drawing or reception room, with furniture of bird's-eye maple covered with rich damask. Out of this opened the dining-hall. . . . Opposite this was a smaller apartment, the usual dining-hall of the family; next adjoining were the china-room and offices, with coach house and barn behind. At the left of the entrance was a second saloon, or family drawing-room."

The house was occupied by the British during the Revolutionary War but the only damage by the soldiers was from the thrusting of swords through the fences and the breaking of windowpanes.

View of the Common, 1708, after a water color by Christian
Remick engraved by Sidney Smith, 1904, showing the
Hancock House and the beacon on Beacon Hill

John Hancock entertained elaborately here and was
a generous host. After the British left, Lafayette was his
guest in 1781 and about forty French officers dined there
every day. According to Madam Hancock, "the Common
was bedizened with lace" and the cooks were driven to
despair. Some say they milked the cows on the Common,
their own and others, to get enough milk.

Hancock intended to give his home to the Common-
wealth to be used as a museum of the Revolution or as a

18th century Colonial interior of Mount Pleasant, *Philadelphia, of the type also found in Boston at this time*

governor's mansion, but he died while making his will. The family offered it later but it was not accepted and all efforts to save this beautiful and historic colonial house failed. It was torn down in 1863.

There were a few other grand houses in Boston in the colonial period, not previously mentioned. Sir Charles Henry Frankland's mansion was on Garden Court in the North End. This was a three-and-a-half-story house of brick with twenty-six rooms, inlaid floors, and richly carved mantels and stairs.

*18th century Colonial Staircase in the Derby House, Salem,
of the type also used in Boston at this time*

Next door was Governor Hutchinson's mansion house. He was Cotton Mather's brother-in-law and lived near him in the North End. His large brick house was handsomely furnished and he possessed a valuable library. Both of these houses were later torn down.

Shirley Place, *a Colonial Governor's Mansion, built 1748 by Governor William Shirley on Roxbury Hill*

Another fine mansion still stands on * Roxbury Hill. Built by Governor Shirley about 1748, this stately home was known as ** Shirley Place. Here the popular royal governor lived, entertained many distinguished guests, and labored for understanding between England and the colo-

Entrance door at Shirley Place

Window seat
at *Shirley Place*

nies. His interests were widespread and not confined to his duties as governor of Massachusetts. He knew the people and the country well, having come over here ten years before he became governor in 1741. As commander-in-chief of the British forces in America before the Revolution, he was a great leader and strategist, and distinguished himself in the capture of Louisburg when the French were driven out in 1745.

William Shirley was loyal both to the Crown and to the colonies and deeply interested in the welfare and prosperity of the latter. It is hoped that his historic Governor's Mansion, known today as the Shirley-Eustis House, will soon be restored to its former dignity.

116

In the late colonial period when Boston had grown and prospered, history was in the making. The colonists resented the English control but they sent to England for luxuries, built their homes in the Georgian style and lived in the manner of the British. They were loyal to the King until George III came to the throne and then the trouble began in earnest.

In 1765 Colonel Barre, in a speech delivered in the English Parliament, called the opposing colonists in Boston the "Sons of Liberty." These patriots met under a great elm tree which stood in an open space called Hanover Square, now the intersection of * Boylston, Washington, and Essex streets. This elm tree became the "Liberty Tree" and on it were hung the effigies of the detested British officials. ** A plaque on a building now marks this site.

Liberty Tree, 1774, from an old print

Portrait of Paul Revere (1734-1818) by John Singleton Copley

When these meetings of the Sons of Liberty became more frequent and important, the British soldiers cut down this tree. A "Liberty Pole" was set up in its place.

** A large silver punch bowl was ordered by fifteen Sons of Liberty in 1768 and was made by Paul Revere. This "Liberty Bowl" is now one of the treasures of the Museum of Fine Arts.

Copied in all sizes today, this symbol of resistance to tyranny is familiar to all Americans as the "*Paul Revere bowl.*" We should remember the significance of the Sons

The Liberty Bowl by Paul Revere

of Liberty and the importance of the Liberty Tree. Let us heed the words of Lafayette, "The world should never forget the spot where once stood Liberty Tree."

The Liberty Tree plaque, site of the Liberty Tree, on a building at the end of Boylston Street on Washington Street

A SUGGESTED TOUR
OF COLONIAL BOSTON

for the hurried, intelligent traveler

BEGIN BY taking a taxi to the PAUL REVERE HOUSE in North
Square. After visiting the house proceed on foot to the HITCH-
BORN HOUSE, which is next door. Visit this house, then walk
via Prince Street to Salem Street to the OLD NORTH CHURCH.
After visiting this church walk up Hull Street to Copp's Hill and
the BURYING GROUND. While there, enjoy the view of the
U.S.S. CONSTITUTION berthed at the Navy Yard, and also the
BUNKER HILL MONUMENT.

Return down Hull Street to the OLD NORTH CHURCH and
walk behind the church to the Paul Revere Mall with its eques-
trian statue of the patriot by Cyrus E. Dallin. Then proceed on
down Hanover Street under the elevated highway to Dock Square
to FANEUIL HALL. Visit this fine building and proceed to
Union Street across Adams Square to the CAPEN HOUSE now
the OLDE OYSTER HOUSE restaurant. Then walk on to the
nearby BOSTON STONE. Then via Marshall Street to the
EBENEZER HANCOCK HOUSE and from there to the OLD
STATE HOUSE via Adams Square and Devonshire Street. Then
to the OLD SOUTH CHURCH a short distance down Washington Street, past the OLD CORNER BOOK STORE on the corner
of School Street, up to KING'S CHAPEL at School and Tremont
streets and the FIRST BURYING GROUND beside it, to the
old GRANARY BURYING GROUND down Tremont Street
and on to THE COMMON and the CENTRAL BURYING
GROUND on the Boylston Street side to the site of the LIBERTY
TREE at the end of Boylston Street on Washington Street.

Finally take a taxi or subway via Huntington Avenue car to
THE MUSEUM OF FINE ARTS to see colonial portraits, furniture and silver, including the PAUL REVERE BOWL.

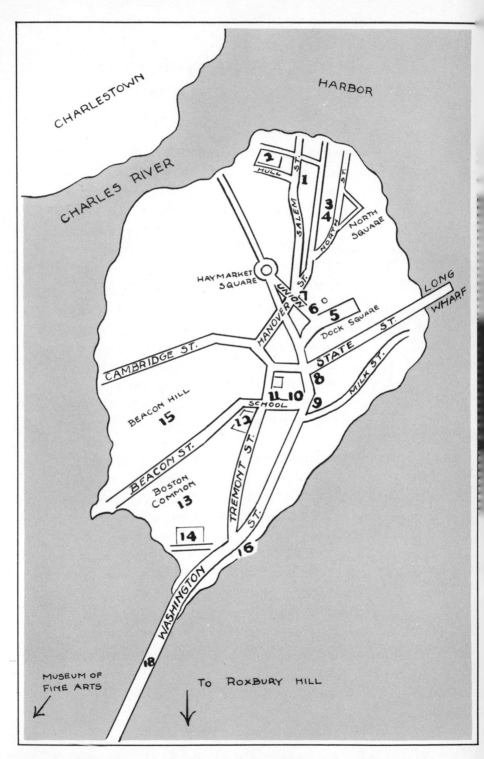

MAP of colonial Boston with historic sites indicated

HISTORIC SITES

Indicated on map of colonial Boston

1—Christ Church, the "Old North Church"
2—Copp's Hill and the Burying Ground
3—The Paul Revere House
4—The Moses Pierce-Hichborn House
5—Faneuil Hall
6—The Capen House
7—The Boston Stone and the Hancock House
8—The Old State House
9—The Old South Meeting house
10—The Old Corner Bookstore
11—King's Chapel and the First Burying Ground
12—The Old Granary Burying Ground
13—The Common
14—The Central Burying Ground
15—Beacon Hill
16—Site of the Liberty Tree

SOME HISTORIC SITES
NEAR BOSTON

(For routes, see any good road map)

CONCORD   *About 20 miles northwest of Boston*
The Battleground and the Bridge
The Concord Antiquarian Society, Museum Rooms and Collections
The Wright Tavern, 1747
The Old Manse, 1769, and many other 18th and 19th
  century houses
The homes of Emerson, Hawthorne and Louisa May Alcott

LEXINGTON   *About 20 miles northwest of Boston*
The Green and the Minuteman statue
The Hancock-Clark House, 1698, altered in 1734
The Buckman Tavern, Ca. 1710
The Munroe Tavern, 1695, altered in the 18th century

SALEM   *About 20 miles northeast of Boston*
The Pioneer Village, a replica of the 17th century houses and life
The Essex Institute, Museum collections and houses
Beautiful 17th, 18th and 19th century houses including the
   following
        The House of Seven Gables, the Derby House, the Pierce-
        Nichols House, The Gardner-Pingree House (the two
        latter by Samuel McIntire)
The Peabody Museum, Marine Collection and East India
memorabilia

PLYMOUTH   *About 30 miles southeast of Boston*
Plymouth Rock
Burial Ground
Mayflower II
Pilgrim Hall, Museum collections
Charming 17th, 18th and 19th century houses
Plimouth Plantation, a replica of Pilgrim houses and life

QUINCY   *About 8 miles southeast of Boston*
Birthplaces of John Adams and John Quincy Adams, 2nd and 6th
   presidents
The Adams Mansion
The Quincy Homestead (Home of Dorothy, who married John
   Hancock)

SAUGUS   *About 10 miles north of Boston*
17th century Ironworks, restored
17th century houses, including the Scotch-Boardman House

INDEX

Ann Street, 48
Armorial markers, Copp's Hill
  Burying ground, 43
Ancient and Honorable Artillery
  Company, 37, 64, 89, 90
Avery, Richard, 81

Beacon Hill, 25, 32, 56, 108
Beacon pole, Ill. 55, 56
Bells, church, 78, 100
Blackstone, Rev. William, 25, 35
Book of Possessions, 31, 42
Boston, 31, 32, 33, Ill. 33, 44, 56,
  60, 61
Boston Athenaeum, 33
Boston Common, 35, 36, Ill. 36
Boston Harbor, 25, 40, Ill. 38
Boston Latin School, 56
Boston Stone, 46, Ill. 46
Boston Tea Party, 71, 98
Bostonian Society, 47, 70, Ill. 70,
  98
Bricks, American, 61, 75
Brick Church, North End, 49
Buildings, brick, 49, 58, 61, Ill. 62,
  64, 67, Ill. 69, 71, Ill. 71, 72,
  Ill. 74, 75, 82, Ill. 83
Buildings, stone, 90, 100, 110
Bulfinch, Charles, 78, 88
Bunch-of-Grapes Tavern, 72
Burying grounds, 33, 34, 43, 105,
  107

Cabot, John, 26
Capen House, 64, Ill. 65, 66, 67
Cemetery, First, 33, 34, Ill. 34
Central Burial Ground, Ill. 106,
  107
Charles River, 25, 44
Charlestown, 25, 33, 44
Charter Street, 54
Child, Thomas, 47

Christ Church, the "Old North
  Church," 75, 78, Ill. 79. Ill. 80,
  81, 82
Church, First, 34
Church, New Brick, 49, 61
Church, Old South Meeting
  House, 82, Ill. 83, Ill. 84, 85, 86
Church, silver, 35, Ill. 35, 82,
  104, 105
Churches, wooden, Ill. 48, 49,
  Ill. 55, 56
Clark Square, 48
Clough, Ebenezer, 75
Colonial sites, 33, 40, 43, 46, 51,
  52, 53, 61, 64, 67, 72, 75, 82,
  86, 95, 100, 105, 107, 108, 117
Colonial South End, 31, 45
Copley, John Singleton, Ill. 108,
  108, Ill. 109, 109, Ill. 118
Copp's Hill, 32, 42, 43, 44
Copp's Hill Burying Ground,
  Ill. 42, 43, Ill. 43
Cornhill Street, 40
Cradle of Liberty, 89, 98
Cresse, Thomas, 72

Dock Square, 45, 55, 87
Drowne, Shem, 58, Ill. 59, 78,
  Ill. 88, 89
Duc de Chartres, Louis-Philippe,
  67

Faneuil Hall, 87, Ill. 87, 88, Ill.
  88, 89
Faneuil Mansion, 90, 91, 92, 93,
  94
Faneuil, Household inventory,
  91, 92, Ill. 93, 94
Faneuil, Peter, 86, Ill. 92, 103,
  105
Ferry, 44
Fires, 49, 96, Ill. 84

Fort Hill, 32, 40
Frankland, Sir Charles Henry, 112
Franklin, Benjamin, 31, 56, 67, 70, 85
Franklin, Josiah, 70, Ill. 70, 105

General Court, 33, 35, 40, 44, 61
Gorges, Robert, 25
Green Dragon Tavern, 71

"Half-timber" style buildings, Ill. 20, 31, 37, 52, 53, Ill. 54, 55
Hancock, Ebenezer, 67
Hancock House, Beacon Street, 110, Ill. 111, 112
Hancock House, Marshall Street, 67, Ill. 69, 110, Ill. 111, 111, 112
Hancock, John, 105, Ill. 108, 109, 111
Harrison, Peter, 100
Harvard College, 20
Hichborn House, Moses Pierce-, 61, Ill. 62, Ill. 63, 64
Household furnishings, 28, 49, 64, 90
Historic landmarks, 33, 82, Ill. 83, 87, Ill. 87, Ill. 88, 95, Ill. 96, Ill. 98, 98
Houses, Ill. 20, Ill. 21, 25, 26, 27, 29, Ill. 29, Ill. 30, 31, 40, 49, 51, 52, Ill. 52, 53, Ill. 53, 58, 61, Ill. 62, 65, 67, Ill. 69, 110, Ill. 111, 112, 114, Ill. 115, 116
Hull, Hannah, 44
Hull, John, 43
Hull Street, 43, 44
Hutchinson, Anne, 72

Interiors, Ill. 21, 26, 28, 47, 58, 61, 62, 67, 70, 110, Ill. 112, 112, Ill. 113, 114, Ill. 114, Ill. 115, Ill. 116, 117
Ironworks, Saugus, 21, Ill. 20, 21

Jeffs, John, 51, 61

Jenks, Joseph, 44
Julien, 107

Keayne, Captain Robert, 37
King's Chapel, 34, Ill. 55, 56, 100, Ill. 101, Ill. 102, 102, 103, Ill. 103, 104
King Street, 34, 37, 40, 95

Lafayette, Marquis de, 72, 89, 120
Liberty Bowl, 119, Ill. 119, 120
Liberty Tree, 117, Ill. 117, 120, Ill. 120
Longfellow, Henry Wadsworth, 78
Louisburg Square, 25

Maps of Boston, Ill. 6, 7, Ill. 22, 26, Ill. 38, 39, Ill. 76, 77, Ill. 122
Market Place, 35
Marlborough Street, 58
Marshall Street, 45, Ill. 45, 46, 47
Massachusetts Bay Colony, 25, 31, 56, Ill. 91
Massachusetts Historical Society, 58, Ill. 59, 60
Mather, Cotton, 43, 49, Ill. 50
Mather, Increase, 43, Ill. 43, 49, 51
Mather, tomb, Copp's Hill Burying Ground, Ill. 43
Mayflower, II, 26, 27, Ill. 27
Milk Street, 25, 58, 82
Mill Creek, 45
Mill Field, 42
Mill Pond, 44
Mount Vernon, 32
Museum of Fine Arts, Boston, 35, Ill. 51, 51, 59, Ill. 84, Ill. 109, 109, Ill. 118, 119, Ill. 119
Mystic River, 25

Navy Yard, Charlestown, 44
Neck, 38, 39
Newspapers, 72, Ill. 73

North End, 40, 45, 49, 51, 75
North Square, 48, Ill. 48, 49, 51

Old Corner Book Store, 72,
    Ill. 74
Old Feather Store, Ill. 54, 55
Old Granary Burying Ground,
    105, 106
Olde Oyster House, Ill. 65, 67
Old North Church, North
    Square, Ill. 48, 49, 51
Old South Meeting House, 58,
    82, Ill. 83, Ill. 84, 85, 86
Old State House, 37, 40, 72, 95,
    Ill. 95
Otis, James, 89, 105

Pemberton Hill, 32
Plimoth Plantation, 26
Pine Tree Shilling, 43, Ill. 44
Plymouth, 26, 124
Price, William, 75
Province House, Ill. 57, 58,
    Ill. 59, 60

Revere, Joseph Warren, 78
Revere, Paul, 40, 44, 50, 51, 53,
    54, 72, 100, 105, 109, Ill. 118,
    119, Ill. 119
Revere, Paul, house, 40, 51, 52,
    Ill. 53, 54, 61
Revere, Paul, bowl, 119, Ill. 119,
    120
Roxbury Hill, 114
Royal Governor's residence,
    114, Ill. 114, Ill. 115, Ill. 116
Rumford, Count, 66, Ill. 66

Salem Street, 75
Second Church, original old
    north, 49, Ill. 48
Sentry Hill, Ill. 55, 56
Sergeant, Peter, 58

Sewall, Judge Samuel, 34, 44,
    47, Ill. 51, 105
Shawmut, 32
Shirley-Eustis House, Ill. 114,
    114, 116, Ill. 116
Shirley, Governor William, 78,
    100, 103, 114, 116
Shops, 40, 49
Signs, trade, 42
Smibert, John, Ill. 51, 88, Ill. 91
Snow Hill, 42
Society for the Preservation of
    New England Antiquities, 30
Sons of Liberty, 117, 119,
    Ill. 119, 120
Spring Lane, 25
State House, old, 37, 40, 72
State Street, 25, 35, 72
Streets, earliest, 25, 34, 35, 37,
    40, 45, 46, 47, 48, 49, 64, 67,
    70, 75, 87, 95, 117, Ill. 120
Stuart, Gilbert, 107, Ill. 107

Taverns, 49, 71, Ill. 71, 72
Thatched buildings, 26, 28,
    Ill. 29, Ill. 48
Town Cove, 44, 45, 87
Town Dock, 44, 45
Town House, 37, Ill. 37
Trimountain, 32

Union Street, Ill. 45, 47, 64, 71

Washington, George, 72, 89, 100
Washington Street, 25, 35, 40,
    58, 82, 117, Ill. 120
Weather vanes, 50, 58, Ill. 59
Wharves, 40, 44, 49, Ill. 76-77,
    Ill. 81, 96, 109
Windmill, 42, 43
Winthrop cup, 35, Ill. 35
Winthrop, Governor John, 24,
    Ill. 24, 33, 85